# MY INTROVERT JOURNEY TO BEING VISIBLE

Join me on my journey from hiding in the shadows full of fear to Sky TV and beyond

**MICHAEL BRIAN MCDONNELL**

Copyright © Michael Brian McDonnell

ISBN: 9798692968883

All rights reserved.
No part of this book may be reproduced in any form or by any electronic or mechanical means, including information storage and retrieval systems, without written permission from the author, except for the use of brief quotations in a book review.

# Dedication

To everyone that never lost faith in me, even when I lost faith in myself.
To everyone that told me to never give up, even when I wanted to.
To my family and friends near and far that stood by me through everything.
To the tough love I received in order to push myself to new heights.

Thank You

To everyone that doesn't feel ready, but acts anyway
To the "quiet people" that feel destined for more
To everyone that has bad days, I have them too
To everyone that wants to break free of the labels and expectations of others
To everyone who's ever doubted themselves
To those that always find something to worry about, even when something good happens

I'm with you.
I see you.

I would also like to dedicate this book to my family, without them I would never have got this far and you would never have this book in your hands.

Thank you for always believing in me, for giving me the space to become who I am today and for being my biggest cheerleader in life.

We did this, together!

*Michael Brian McDonnell*

# Content

| | |
|---|---|
| Introduction | 6 |
| I've Always Felt Different | 13 |
| Searching For Validation And Permission | 50 |
| This Changed My Life Forever | 92 |
| My Public Speaking Journey | 119 |
| Public Speaking Round 2 | 144 |
| Finding Meaning Again | 152 |
| How Could Being Visible Look For You | 185 |
| Join The Community! | 187 |

# Introduction

Looking back, I have almost no clue how I got to where I am today; sat here, writing this book for you. It's one thing to go through life, overcoming your obstacles as everyone does, but then to sit down and put them all together in a book that you just know will benefit others that are going through similar struggles to what I went through; is a very surreal moment for me.

I had to grow up very quickly being diagnosed with Cystic Fibrosis when I was two months old. Yes, my parents did everything and gradually gave me more and more control over looking after myself, but they do that anyway don't they? When you look around and see your friends that don't have to do the same things as you, they don't have to worry about the same things as you and you have to take time off school for hospital appointments and operations and a whole host of other things I needed to do to get by when I was younger; the story of "not being good enough" quickly sets in firmly in my mind.

I was a happy go lucky child, always either playing games, running around and just enjoying everything and making fun. I think deep down, in the beginning, because of the conditions, everyone had this "you don't know how long I had left" so didn't put a lot of pressure on me to be great at something and used, "do what you want to do" as the guiding light for my life moving forward.

This caused me to look at things very differently, think differently and want to not do things that other people did. I had the ability to take an outside perspective and make choices based on what I really wanted to do. Which led me to running my own business rather than getting a job and working for someone else. This allowed me to look after myself health wise and earn enough money to live the life I wanted to live; which led me to tennis coaching.

I stumbled into tennis unexpectedly, my brother started playing before I did and encouraged me to try it and said, "you never know, you might like it;" which I did. This kept me fit, kept me occupied and I started to compete locally and gradually got better all the time. One day, the coach I had noticed that while I was competing nationally for my university, that I also had the knack for motivating the other players and asked me if I would consider becoming a coach; my response was, "I'll give it a go, yeah."

This is the, "and the rest is history" moment but I do want to share what it was like to help someone improve for the first time, which gave me the motivation and purpose which leads me to, over ten years later, writing the book you have in your hands right now.

When I first started coaching tennis I was roughly fifteen years old; and when you're young, trying to do something new for the first time, you volunteered to "earn your stripes" to gradually prepare yourself for being a coach full time. So, naturally, I started out assisting the head coach, coaching children. One of the moments I'll never forget was helping a boy hit the ball and keep it on the tennis court for the first time, he was around five years old. The look of shock, happiness and excitement across his face was indescribable for me; his laugh and my smile filled me with a sense of "YES! I did that!" which of course was me helping him, but he actually hit the ball. The first thing that came to my mind was that I had to go and pick up the tennis balls; but after that it was such a happy thought of, "I'd love to do this all the time, this is amazing!"

And the rest is history...

What happened next was a series of things that led to me becoming a self employed tennis coach; then when I realised that helping people lose weight and feeling great about themselves felt like a BIGGER mission than tennis, I felt pulled to become a personal trainer (crazy I know, health and fitness professional with health conditions) which all stemmed from this desire to help people, to chase the feel good feeling, and realising that I was actually good at something others struggled with, so felt compelled to help them.

My desire for helping people, being of service, contributing to the greater good, burned me out eventually; I hit bottom. Tennis coaching, personal training, my own workouts, my treatments, having time to eat, relax, destress and look after myself... took its toll. I couldn't sleep properly, I couldn't really commit to my own workouts or eat enough to really recover properly. And being diagnosed as diabetic in my twenties (it's related to my cystic fibrosis so wasn't because I didn't look after myself... more on that later on in the book) flipped the script on what I knew worked, my diet had to change, my exercise had to change; my entire life and what I knew worked for me had to change. Which also took its toll on me.

That's what this book is about; contributing at the highest level for you in a way that doesn't take away from your own happiness and zest for life. It was after burning out and realizing that this could be an opportunity in disguise, being diagnosed with diabetes made me feel like I can't play small anymore, I can't mess around as I just don't know how long I have. I also did the stupid thing of looking up the mortality rate of someone with cystic fibrosis and cystic fibrosis related diabetes.... I realised I was on "borrowed time" as I was older than the number on the screen... so I got to work.

The aim of this book is to give you a real sense of what I've gone through as an introvert -the major turning points of my life that you probably aren't aware of- to really get "inside my head" and take aspects of what I did into your own life. Today I host my top-rated self improvement podcast "The Ask Mike Show" where I've interviewed celebrities, experts, icons and inspirations around the world, I've spoken on stages in multiple countries and host my own events, I'm regularly interviewed on podcasts and featured in the media... But it wasn't always that way and I've nearly always "acted scared" or acted before I felt ready.

In this book you'll learn where I've come from and what I've gone through, but you'll also get a peak behind the curtain of someone that not just teaches it, not just helps people with putting themselves out there and overcoming the mental battles... but lives it too!

It's time to learn what it's actually like.

## I've Always Felt Different

There's nothing quite like being told from as young as you can remember that you're always going to be different, probably never going to ever fit in or be the same as the other children; That you might never really amount to anything and that you're going to be taking everyday as it comes. Of course, They never said that directly; kind, caring people that only want the best for you never do; but that's how it felt for me. At the start, it was my parents taking 99.99% of the responsibility and I'll forever be thankful, grateful and secretly guilty for that as I'll never be able to repay them for everything they've ever done for me.

Failing to thrive as a baby and doctors asking, "do you want to save this child?"... I can only imagine what went through their minds at the time and you're only reading this book because they said, "yes." They signed up for at least sixteen to eighteen years of having to go beyond expectations everyday. Looking after me, near constant hospital appointments, operations, making me do things neither them nor me wanted to go through. It was hard for them as much as it was for me because as much as I actually had to go through those things (and the more aware of what was happening I was, the worse it was), they had to actually sit and watch me, near powerless, and accept that as long as I get through it, as long as I "make it," that we can get back to living our lives again.

So I'd be lying if I said that for the first decade it was just me going through this; because it wasn't.

But as I got older, I realised just how hard it was to not only live with cystic fibrosis and diabetes (and its effects) but also do what needs to be done in terms of treatments, medicines and lifestyle so I can not only get through each day, but thrive each day, to be in a position whereby I can start to plan for the future because I felt I had one, to feel safe enough to go beyond the day to day... while living with the unpredictable bad days, the lack of energy whilst not being able to just feel better by having an energy drink or sugar due to the repercussions.

To really, really learn just what I've gone through, and how it's shaped me, you will need to learn the ins and outs of what it was like for me. You'll need to come with me from the beginning to learn what broke me, the moments of "I've had enough," and I'll also take you through the conversations, the exercises and ways of thinking that got me through it in the hope that you can take these and implement them in your own lives.

Taking you all the way to the beginning, there will be some dark moments, emotional moments, but I feel that this is the best and only way to help you the best way I can.

Going all the way back, school was where it started for me; I was a happy go lucky kid in the United Kingdom, that enjoyed to run, make up fantasies and generally have a laugh. I enjoyed sport and keeping active through football, races, martial arts, PE amongst other things.... But I had a secret.

I knew I was different; behind closed doors I had treatments, medicines and physio that I needed to do just to feel "normal" that the majority of the other children didn't need to do. I would wake up, and the first thing I would do was my physio (when I was younger it would be my parents doing that) and I'd go downstairs to have breakfast. Before I would even eat anything I would need to prepare my medicines (which would be tablets, nebulisers and inhalers) that I would also need to take... then I would eat; and I would do these twice a day.

Now, at first it seems like it's not so bad, that it was easy to do these things then go about my day, and you would be right; if there wasn't more to it. When you're younger you pick up on everything, consciously and subconsciously, which meant the looks I'd get taking my tablets in school, the feeling I'd get when I started to get tired before the other children.

But, again, when you're younger and you just do as you're told because it's the best chance I've got at preventing my condition from worsening, you do it, no questions asked; because you have to. There was one moment when It really hit me that I was different, that I felt a little too different, and that caused me to adjust who I was… and it was something called "Jeans for Jeans day."

Jeans for Jeans day was a fundraising event that the CF Trust endorses which involves wearing jeans to school to help raise money for cystic fibrosis. When we put the idea to my primary school they of course said yes but organised it as a non-uniform day instead of just jeans in case some didn't wear jeans but wanted to still participate. So we set the date, organised the posters, newsletters and flyers and the whole school got involved, infants and juniors as they were called.

What was part of the event was giving the children a story about what the event is about, why are they allowed to wear normal clothes today? ... which involved organising an assembly and me having to stand up in front of the whole school and share about my condition, how it effects me and why their donations are going to a good cause.

Picture it, a little boy who's kept his little secret from pretty much the entire school aside from his best friends, has to stand up in front of the whole school, talk about his health conditions, talk about the tablets he takes, the treatments and how the condition affects him. As of writing this, it was a long time ago, but I still remember the faces staring at me, the way I could only really focus on the teacher asking me questions and praying I say the right thing.

Nervous, singled out, shaking, in the spotlight in a way most children simply don't want to happen to them... anxious doesn't even cover it; I was full on afraid. From that point on, I knew I was different, there was no support group for people with cystic fibrosis as we could "cross infect" which meant I was the only child in the school that was allowed to have this condition. I felt too different, the worst in the room as cystic fibrosis was a disease, it wasn't a good thing to have.

Did I connect the dots in an overly negative way? My short answer is not yet. After that day things simply went back to normal, despite me wondering if standing up meant things would forever change for me.

Have you ever felt like after you put your head above the rest and put yourself in the spotlight that your life would forever change?

Make the repercussions so big and scary that you always feel like things will never be the same?

Well, that is what I did, but in reality, school was back to normal, just another day and the world spins on. So if you ever feel like things will be way bigger and life defining than they actually are, you're not alone and sometimes we have to realise that we make things so much bigger inside our own heads than they actually are and use that to help reduce the anxiety about the situation in order to wrap our head around the fact that it's not a "big deal" in the end.

One of the things that did imprint on me was just how scary it was to be singled out, to be put on a pedestal and judged. I felt horrible, the worst in the entire school of hundreds. It's hard to describe as now, looking back, this did play a part because it was the first time I really noticed it. I was at a time in my life when I just wanted to be the same as everyone else, I just wanted to fit in, get through my day, and the treatments I needed to do twice a day enabled me to do that. To have my "secret," the thing I kept to myself and did behind closed doors, out in the open for all to see... was embarrassing. That combined with the feeling of being worse than everyone else in the school was something I carried with me.

It wasn't about the event, it wasn't about being up in the assembly; it was about how it made me feel at the time and what I meant for me doing that. So think, what have you done in your past that might seem unimportant? You might have brushed it aside in your own mind, but it played a part in shaping your belief system as it's what It meant to you and how it made you feel.

## HIGH SCHOOL

This was one of the hardest and darkest moments of my life; I know, slight over exaggeration given what else I'll be talking about in this book, but at the time it was. As soon as I stepped foot in my new school I realised how big everything was, how different and initially it hit me. I was fairly quiet and had a hard time making friends. I barely saw my old friends (it was like the schedules never lined up) and some went to different schools.

I became the child that wouldn't talk to you unless you spoke to me first. I would think about what to say, then by the time I felt like I could actually say the words, the time passed and it was no longer relevant. Makes me chuckle saying it now as I'm a completely different person in the right situation, but I still have that mode. I still have the sense of, "can I say this?" to this day and I think it comes from my time growing up. So many different voices all trying to be heard and sometimes someone else would say what I wanted to say so thought "Well I don't need to say anything now."

It was at this phase of my life that I was picked on because of my looks, nearly everyday the little comments would come in and remind me of how lesser and smaller I was compared to them. It was never terrible, I don't want to give you the impression that I had a horrible time, but it was everyday name calling and laughing which just chipped away at my worth as a person, downgrading myself to a thing versus a person. Whenever I would start to feel like I could relax, the names would start again. I felt on edge, couldn't relax, and I got to the point where I just kept to myself, went inside my shell and had no reason to come out. What made things worse for me was that I stayed in my shell to avoid the potential negative, to avoid the potential name calling, or making fun, or me doing or saying the wrong thing.

Then I found people that gave me positive feedback for doing things they wanted me to do, teachers, so I started to pay attention, do the work, do as I was told. But because I also had the negativity, I became drawn to the idea of pleasing the teachers and I started to go the extra mile with the things I was also good at. The best example of this was maths; I got to the point where I would ask for extra homework, doing work that was two or three years ahead of me because I got told I was good, "well done." It felt good at a time when I got little positivity. I kept things to myself at home too and I just went through the motions of treatments, medicines, food, homework, listen to music or watch films, then I'd go to sleep to wake up and do it all over again.

So, I avoided the negativity as much as possible by keeping to myself and being in my shell, I was drawn to the positivity and pleasing the teachers. I spent so long doing that that it actually started to get easy......

That is what became dangerous for me, which at the time, I had no idea what was happening. It's so easy writing this book, looking back, and saying that it was a bad thing for hiding in the shadows to become easy and actually feel better with my own company than the company of people that didn't really value me as much as I'd like. That's the benefit of hindsight; but remember this, things becoming comfortable, easy, when they're unhealthy or simply making yourself miserable; is the way you might be living right now. There's always a moment when the pain of staying the same is greater than the potential pain of change; if that's where you are right now then don't wait for things to get so bad before you change them.

There's a chance that I should have taken responsibility myself for the way things were. I had friends, good friends, but I just valued quality of friendships with people that actually valued me enough to respect me. It's strange how young I was when I was aware enough of myself to realise that that was what I wanted instead of the superficial friendships with people that only liked me If I was similar to them. Realising my difference and how wanting to just be myself played a huge part in how I developed as a human. I wasn't prepared to sacrifice or change who I was to fit in and that did lead to me not really fitting in at all; which at the time wasn't very enjoyable, but now I'm actually proud of my younger self for not changing too much just to fit in.

So in some ways, I was proud of the way I held on to who I was.... Or did I? Or did I simply get to the point where it was "normal?" Accepting that hiding, being in the shadows and being invisible was "just the way it is" and completely normal was a sign that I'd fallen down the trap of pleasing people and doing whatever it took just to get by.... Even if that meant I was miserable. So you see, your mind can play tricks on you and convince you that you're doing the right thing.

It was a crazy feeling when you either feel miserable, sad, anxious, afraid... or nothing. I cut myself off. I rationalised it to myself that It actually felt better to feel nothing at all than the alternative. It was at this stage of my life that I realised that I'd developed this detachment from emotions and living with that simply made going through the motions easier while I had no real desire for anything. I didn't feel motivated to change anything; because in order to do that I'd have to go through the negative, "go through the dark to get to the light" so to speak and it wasn't something I was prepared to face at the time as I didn't need to. Maybe this is something you can relate to?

What I noticed was, at the time, I had no desire to go through the uncomfortable to get to the stage where I was happier, more at peace and actually moving towards what I wanted. Something I'll talk about later on; but this is often the case where big changes are hard and uncomfortable first, but once you get through that, you'll be glad you did. Preventing the negative from happening doesn't mean you start to feel good, feeling good is something you have to actively go after.

**I LOST MYSELF**

It was after all that, when I looked back over what happened to me and how I felt, that I realised that I forgot who I was in this pursuit of pleasing others. Doing so much for others, getting the positive feedback for doing what others wanted and negativity when I didn't. That, combined with the name calling and realising that I naturally tried to avoid the negativity for years meant that I didn't realise who I was and what would make me happy; what I wanted to do. I was at the stage of my life when I had to make decisions about my life, decisions about what I wanted to do at a time when I was in the most fragile and confused time of my life so far.

I had absolutely no clue what I wanted to do; plus, I spent so long looking outside myself (friends, family, teachers, bullies) that I'd lost my own voice and the ability to listen to it. I'd lost the trust and belief in myself that you need to be able to make decisions for yourself. I didn't know who I was anymore, didn't know who to be or who I wanted to be. I was lost.

I started to ask myself a lot of questions, and if you've ever been in a space where you've been people pleasing, chasing other's happiness while sacrificing your own, then maybe these questions will help you too:

Who are you without trying to please others all the time?

Who are you without people telling you how to think and act?

What would you do even if it meant you lost friends?

Who do you want to be?

I asked myself these questions on my own, in a room, just me and a notepad. I would sit there staring at the questions until I answered them and made sure I did answer them. No backing out, no distractions. It was one of the most confusing times of my life and I needed to get out of this, I needed to. I'd read a few personal development books at this point because I needed to deal with the day to day goings on as a teenager too. Consider that I'm also changing at a rapid rate with hormones and the like along with all of this going on too!

I was hoping that these questions would help me realise who I was without others, without the bullies, and even without the positive too because I lived for pleasing people at the same time as not doing things others didn't want. Asking difficult questions like "who do I want to be?" took me weeks before I could actually answer it. I would spend days and days staring at the question thinking, "I have absolutely no idea!" and all kinds of thoughts would run through my head about not answering it. I considered binning the piece of paper and never looking at it again many times (it reminds me of withdrawal symptoms) calling myself all the names under the sun for not being able to answer a simple question. But the simple questions are often the hardest to answer; and it was only after answering the difficult questions that I was able to realise that sport, coaching was the thing I wanted to pursue.

**COLLEGE**

College was a completely different experience for me. It was like I had been picked out of one of the worst experiences of my life and put into one of the best (at the time) within a year. It took me a while to get used to the idea of being liked. I had a strange sense of confidence after realising who I wanted to be and I had the feeling of "ok, this can be your fresh start, Mike." It was like I drew a line in the sand of my old life and quickly had the opportunity to remake myself at college.

One of the first things I noticed was that there was less instant judgement in a negative way. It was like they wanted to get to know each other more in college and were a lot more reasonable. I always remember a moment where I would sit down in the cafe and classmates would sit with me and chat; sounds so small doesn't it? But the fact that they made an effort almost gave me permission to make an effort too because I didn't think It would lead to anything bad. If you remember, I spent a long time preventing the bad things from happening in the first place.

But this was different, I felt safer; having the social circle had a strange effect on me. The only way I could describe it was "pressure;" I felt the pressure release. The safety it created allowed me to do several things

I felt like I could break my routines and experiment with new things; as someone that had a set routine for a lot of things (morning routines, medicines, treatments) -it was helpful and comfortable for maintaining my health- but being able to break something that worked for me for something better and making me happier was one of the hardest things I've ever had to do up until now. Safety had to come first before I felt like I could leave my comfort zone. You hear a lot about comfort zones, the idea that you have to leave your comfort zone before you can change, do more, and be more; but most don't speak about how you have to feel like you can, you have to feel safe to explore the unknown. At moments like these I realise that it was ok to be myself; I wasn't broken, there wasn't anything wrong with me and that I was able to be myself, do what I wanted and what I needed to do at the same time.

It completely changed me, the lack of pressure meant I suddenly started finding myself talking to people without them starting the conversations first -which I always did before- so conversations with friends in the cafe, speaking out during lectures and generally feeling happier day to day; all stemmed from feeling like I belonged a lot more. I was accepted for who I was, respected and treated like an equal, valued, and I felt like I was able to connect with people more than I ever did. All the years before isolating myself in a huge way lead to this feeling like a weight had finally been lifted, The relief I felt was nearly indescribable and it took me all the way back to my happy go lucky self when I was in primary school.

Isn't it funny how that can work? The way we can trace back the transformation and go all the way back to before the negativity happened? I was aware of what was going on while it was happening and it felt weird; like peeling back the layers of who I was and what ever's left before I had to change who I was to cope with what I went through. At first, it was frightening because I had no idea who I am without the pressure anymore; but rather than shy away from it, I leaned into it and went on a journey of self discovery. Discovering the values I have, what beliefs I wanted and how they translated into how I showed up everyday really helped give me the clarity I needed. It cleared a lot of the confusion and made my life much, much simpler.

## TENNIS COACHING

The first taste of running my own business was tennis coaching. After working a saturday job at a tennis club -not enjoying being told what to do as an employee- and volunteering as an assistant tennis coach after that, I thought it was only natural that I would go into tennis coaching full time. Being a self-employed tennis coach seemed to be the only way I was going to make it work out the gate so I committed and got started. Oh boy, was I in for a bit of a shock.

This was the first time that I wasn't just delivering tennis coaching, I needed to be social and get over my fear of talking to strangers, everyone is a stranger at first and I needed to build relationships with the members. This was the real moment when I had to "come out of my own skin" and grow up very quickly if I was going to grow this business.

It was hard, I remember moments when I'd convince myself to talk to people, start to walk up to them, hands sweating, able to hear my heart beating, thinking about what I'd say, then carry on walking because I couldn't think of anything or I just chickened out. I had a long journey of doing that over and over again before I felt even remotely "safe" enough to speak to people. It was made easier if they attended my classes which gave me a bit of a confidence boost when it came to speaking to them, that was the first few months, speaking to the parents of the children or adults who attended my tennis coaching sessions.

At the time I was in my early twenties, still in university and still experiencing the aftermath of the self awareness growth I had during college. This presented its own set of challenges that I didn't realise until then. The main one being that some of the members didn't trust me because I was of a certain age -it was strange to me at first- and it made me think, "ok I have to earn their respect or trust before they would trust that I can help them"; earn my stripes if you will.

I realised that everyone has their own boxes that you need to tick before they'll trust you, everyone has different things they look for and you do need to factor that in when building relationships and selling coaching to them. So I started to enter the member competitions, I kept competing myself, joined in during their club match sessions, went to social events, offered free taster sessions and spent as much time as I could at the club. I knew my stuff, I knew I could help them but I had to show them that I did, I had to keep going until their faith in me matched my faith in me.

It took me a while to realise that but as soon as I started to commit more to building trust and faith in me, everything started to change. Booking clients, having fun and also building loyalty because they felt like they knew me and could trust me because I practiced what I preached. What I didn't realise was that in doing this, I actually increased my own self belief by doing things that instilled belief in others... It was a two way street.

## *PERSONAL TRAINING*

While in university I had a bit of an epiphany; I sat in a lecture on my coach education degree, the lecture was on fitness and how it can enhance the performance of athletes. I was sitting there -twiddling my pen between my hands- and I thought to myself, "hmmmm, fitness plays a huge part in improving my clients' tennis." This caused me to think that I had a handle on my health and fitness even with my health conditions, what if I could help those that are having a hard time with this?

Imagine the ripple effect of helping people become healthier and lose weight! (at this point my head went down the rabbit hole) There and then I decided to become a personal trainer alongside being a tennis coach. I needed to pass the course obviously, but if I did, I would love to change people's lives through being healthier and helping them lose weight. It felt like I was able to then up my game, help more people and give more meaning and purpose to my life.

So, I signed up for a course, passed with flying colours, then I had to figure it out. I had to find a way to be "chatty" when I became a personal trainer. Why? Because there's a difference between wanting to be a personal trainer and doing what it takes in order to actually get clients, something I didn't realise initially. I would just be myself, keeping to myself, delivering the circuit training classes I knew how to teach, then going back to the responsibilities I had. I didn't speak to people unless I had to. I would do all that then realise why I struggled to get clients and customers.

I'll share a story in a minute about the situation that challenged me a lot in this way; but before that I kept quiet and I didn't get results. This meant that sometimes there are simply things you need to do in order to market yourself, put yourself out there and become "desirable" in a way that makes people want to work with you. Again, there is a difference between wanting to provide the service, and what it takes to market yourself and be able to get people to work with. This meant figuring out how to become a performer as such, I had to learn how to be outgoing, chatty, friendly and become the person I needed to be in order to make the business work. The story I'll get into now showcases that

## FIRST SPINNING CLASS

Spinning was the first exercise class I ever instructed where I felt like I was thrown in the deep end right away. This was a massive moment for me because there was a difference (at least in my mind) between tennis coaching which I had been doing since college, and taking an exercise class that was to music and people were copying me. What made things more nerve wracking was that, because it was my first class, I didn't have my own music as it was all organised with short notice; this meant that I had to instruct a class for the first time with someone else's music, and sit at the front of a group of strangers -all eyes on me watching my every move- and push them through a workout.

Now remember, I'm not a loud person, I spent a decade doing my own thing and keeping to myself, so when I work for a gym whereby I have to carry out fitness classes (circuit training I could do) that involve me standing up and performing in front of people, be loud and motivational, telling people what to do, pushing them, entertaining them, and all in all being a completely person to who I've been before; it was something that was very scary for me.

"What would they think of me? What if I say the wrong thing? What if I mess it up? What if I miss a beat on the bike? What if I get a complaint? What if I injure someone?" All these thoughts were swirling around my brain and all I wanted to do was shut the world out and hide in the office, I didn't even want to leave the staff room. And while wearing the mic made it easier for the members to hear me, it also didn't help my fear because it meant that everything I said, they would hear, there was nowhere to hide, no way out, and I was in the spotlight like I never was before.

It was even completely different in my mind to tennis coaching because I had the chance to build my experience first, volunteering and working as an assistant first before I felt comfortable delivering my own sessions. In this case I felt like I was thrown in the deep end.... Which didn't help as I wasn't a very good swimmer.

Anyway, I went out about an hour before to set up my bike and organise the register so I didn't need to do that while everyone was watching with their beady eyes staring at me... then I took my mind off of it by talking to the manager, the staff, other members and generally looking after the gym -I still had an hour- so I still gad things to do which I could use to help reduce my nerves. One of the things I realised was that no matter what you do, sometimes there's no getting around the fact that it's going to be a nerve wracking thing to do. All the breathing, self-talk and walking to get rid of the excess energy can't take your mind away from the facts.

"It's going to be hard, It's going to be difficult, you're going to be nervous... but you can handle it" became my self talk. It wasn't about ignoring the situation, but about understanding it, being ok with it, not hating myself for feeling how I feel and falling back on my ability to handle the situation, trusting myself to be able to "act scared" and do my best. That's the only thing I could control, the only thing I could really be sure of and I needed to allow myself to be nervous, be scared.... But trust that I'll be ok, trust that I can get through it and the results will likely be better because of that. So I got ready early, walked out to the bikes and greeted the members -which helped my nerves-, passed the register around, got myself ready on the bike, introduced myself ... and away I went!

Do you ever have situations where you've been scared, worried or focused on how scary the thing is?

How do you tend to respond?
Does it help?

Maybe, just maybe, it's the trust in yourself and your ability to handle whatever the situation is, your ability to "figure it out" is the only thing that you need in order to take action? Maybe you can use this to your advantage the next time you're in a difficult situation. With there being too many unknowns and things I couldn't control, it's the only thing I had, and maybe the only thing you have too.

After the class, the nerves went -the exercise endorphins helped with that-, did whatever I could do at the time which involved listening to the track for a bit and guessing what everyone could do with the song, and I ended up talking for a little bit after the class was finished. A few of the members got talking to me and I passed a comment about it being my first ever class; they all said that they really enjoyed it, they'd be making sure they attend my classes in the future and that they couldn't tell I was nervous.

There's a lesson in that because it's very often that what we think people think, simply isn't the case in real life; if we could ask everyone we speak to what they think, chances are we'd get very different answers to what we think they're thinking about. They simply didn't know that it was my first class and that I was genuinely nervous and afraid that I was going to mess it up -they couldn't tell I was nervous, I must have carried it off-. So all the worrying, all the stories that I'd created about being bad, them not liking it, me messing up... simply wasn't the case.

I had created this picture in my mind which ultimately did a better job of making me feel horrible and potentially ruining the class, than the actual reality. Something I told myself was, "no one knows how bad I think I am, no one knows that I don't know what I'm doing!" which made me laugh at the time. My advice is, knowing that, we tend to fulfil the expectations or estimations we have of ourselves, or do better in spite of them.

Spending your time believing what you think others think is a wasted effort and you should lean on your trust in your ability to "handle it" and "figure it out" which will lead you to doing the best you can in that situation.

There were many different things that I did where I simply failed -hilariously so- and I decided that I wouldn't do those again. The funniest attempt was a step aerobics class (yes I did attempt it) and I hated it; I couldn't move properly, felt very awkward. I tried a lot of things, some worked, some didn't; and over time I learned what I can pick up easily, what I can learn to get better at and what I should probably be better off not doing again. Tripping over my own feet isn't a good look! Which taught me that it was ok to find your way (to make mistakes) and have things you can start, not be amazing at -at first- so you can then improve. What's interesting is just how you can create a "plan" for yourself around improving at certain things based on doing and reviewing your performance so you can get better.

I spent a long time thinking that I was stuck, I couldn't change and I was the way I was. But looking back, the times I've got through the dark moments were the times I changed myself in some way, I understood that I could do that and took steps. The times when I stayed in the negative space were moments when I wasn't open to the idea of adapting. Changing and growing is a part of getting through your dark times but I need to be open to growing… and if you are ever in situations like this; understanding that you can grow, you can change and that it's OK to do that.

## Searching For Validation And Permission

I spent a long time searching for the validation I needed of my own worth. It was because of my past that I never truly felt like I was good enough or worthy of the things I wanted or desired for myself that was far away from where I was at that moment. It was almost like I had to take small steps or naturally progress and anything outside of that wasn't possible for me. Spending years -decades- having this sense of self doubt made it very difficult for me to ever really stretch my wings and fly in a way that I got more and more frustrated by as I got older. I started to slowly get more and more irritated with myself while at the same time having the belief that I couldn't go after what I wanted. The "push pull" of those mixed feelings slowly started to eat me up alive!

I would sit -staring at my laptop- and see everyone else being able to do amazing things which only made me feel worse; a part of it was comparing myself to them but also another side is that they were doing what they wanted to do while I felt like I couldn't. For some reason they could do these things while I couldn't and that frustrated me even more.

I wanted to impact more people, I wanted to change the world! But I had the conversation of, "but you can't do that, you're not good enough, what makes you think you can do it, who are you to think you can!?" which all kept me stuck for a while until I started to ask myself this question....

What would it take for me to feel like I could?

Now, at first it didn't help. Despite what others may tell you -and told me- about changing the conversation in your head, it isn't an overnight transformation. I spent weeks asking myself that question without any answer at all -I'd draw a blank- and ultimately get frustrated with myself because I didn't have the answers. I knew this was an important question to answer and I simply couldn't figure it out. Looking back I realise I was judging myself too harshly for not being able to do this as quickly as other people, but also because I knew I needed this before I could really go after what I wanted.

I'd journal on it, meditate on it -as best as I could- and I found that over the days of getting nowhere, I started to get less angry at myself and I actually started to find myself brainstorming ideas -even though I couldn't settle on anything- which actually felt like progress to me. Over about three weeks to a month I went from absolutely nothing coming up for me to starting to brainstorming ideas and possible ways I could feel more empowered; ways that I could almost give myself the permission or validation I needed of my own worth and value in this world.

As silly and "wishy washy" as it sounds, I felt like I needed that because I'd been chasing it from teachers to friends to family my entire life; so it was a way of using the way I'm wired to my advantage. Eventually I came up with a few ideas -some a little crazy- that I thought would give me the validation I needed.

Before I dive into these, I need to point out that there was some time between these -they didn't all happen at once- and some of these took me several attempts before I actually got the "yes" I wanted.

## HAVING AN ARTICLE FEATURED IN MAGAZINES

The first thing on my list -that I felt like I could reasonably manage- was being featured in magazines. I was still a tennis coach and personal trainer at the time and I wanted more; I wanted to go bigger than I ever thought I could but I had this fear creeping in too. Writing an article for a magazine was my idea of "dipping my toe in" on the idea of putting myself out there and helping more people with my knowledge, expertise or experience on someone else's platform.

But first, I had to find the online magazines that accept submissions, which was the hard part; spending ages staring at google with no clue what to even search for didn't fill me with confidence. I'd have days where I'd tell myself that It was all a waste of time, I couldn't even find the magazines so how on earth am I ever going to be good enough to actually write an article good enough for them? I would let the fact that I was struggling with step one give me a reason to beat myself up and justify/confirm the story of not being good enough to follow through and get to sending the article. I got to a point where I would look, search and try to find the places to write articles for even though my head was telling me it was pointless and a waste of time.

Eventually I found one. I went on the website, found a section that said "write for us" and I figured that I'd spent a while trying to find this thing -and going through the roller coaster of whether to even do this or not- that I wasn't going to then decide against writing the article. It was a business magazine so I looked at what kind of articles they had featured before including the format and I got to work. I was a personal trainer so I thought I'd approach the article from how health can benefit business owners.

I wrote the article, unsure if it was any good or if it was good enough for them; I did my best -that's all I could do- but I still questioned myself the entire time. Which was absolutely nothing compared to actually going through the process of sending off the article. My brain was in complete "freak out mode" once I actually wrote the article.

I slowly went through their process, my head was telling me I'd get laughed at, told no, and if they said yes and other people hated the article... what then? What if the magazine says yes but everyone that reads it hated it and I'd get a lot of negative comments about it? Could I handle it?

There was secretly a part of me that wanted them to say no -I know, how crazy- because it would confirm to me the stories that I was telling myself the entire time. If they said no then that would mean that I wasn't in fact good enough, that I wasn't ready and that I needed to stick to the things I was always doing without doing anything different. That's the thing, I wanted to be proved right because it meant I didn't need to change -I could stay safe and comfortable- instead of having proof that I could change and I could impact lives at a bigger level. So -much like high school- I wanted to avoid the potential good because I felt I didn't deserve it. I went through all of this while deciding whether to press send on this article or not.

I had to get my emotions under control, I went through a whole detachment process from the outcome along with "turning off" my emotions to a certain extent. I had to start telling myself that "it didn't matter" and that it wasn't important despite it being pretty important to me. There was an element of denial that would come into it in order for me to get into a space where I could handle taking action on the bigger things and detach myself from the outcome. That needed to happen from before, during and after clicking send on the article; it meant a lot to me mentally for me to do this. But I did it, I clicked send on this article.

I suddenly felt relaxed and relieved that I did it -like a weight lifted- and all I could do was sit and wait; I had slowly started to let go of the idea of getting a yes or a no -almost like it didn't matter either way- and I essentially went back to work on my tennis coaching and personal training business as if nothing happened; because I had to. When I got the email from the magazine, my heart froze, time froze and there was a part of me that didn't want to open the email; my finger hovered over the email for a good twenty seconds before I opened it, heart pounding -I could feel my heart beating all around my body- and eventually... took a deep breath in.... And opened it.

I read the email, "We are pleased to inform you that...." and I couldn't believe it! NO WAY! I can't believe that I got my first article featured in a magazine! I was soo giddy -so excited I couldn't sit still- and I shared the article absolutely everywhere for days afterwards. The high I felt was nothing like I had ever experienced before. I did it! Me, all based on what I know and my ability to write. I was in shock.

This was the first time I got the positive recognition for something I did at a bigger level that was about more than just about me. It was feeling a terrifying, horrible feeling and getting the satisfaction of it being worth it -actually worth it- was the first time my "self esteem armour" started to build and strengthen. Sometimes simply getting positive feedback and results can do the world of good for your confidence.

Despite that, I need to fast forward a few months to a time where I actually got a no because it's worth sharing what happened then and the lessons I learned too. Getting the yes, then the no, and what goes into that is important for me to share. I did the whole process again, wrote the article, had the same nerves and fears but submitted anyway. A few days after submitting I got an email, "Unfortunately ...." and my heart sank -it crushed me- and I thought that was it, I was a horrible writer and I should just pack up my laptop and not bother trying again.

I really felt I needed to add that in because learning from the successes is so rare -I did get the validation I needed to dive into the other things- but having the email about not being featured this time made me realise that valuing the good soo much caused the bad triggered me too and took me all the way back to being told no when I was younger and it made me feel like the worst in the world again. I didn't realise that I got so excited and giddy about getting the yes that when I got the no it knocked me more than I would admit at the time -but looking back- I definitely took it to heart more than I thought I did. It took me a while to "recover" -maybe a few days- and get back into writing social media posts and eventually articles again.

While that's something I did -and would hope you didn't copy me- you the reader need to also feel ok with being knocked back; feeling ok with not being happy when something bad happens is human and actually more natural than forcing yourself to feel good even when something bad happens. Feeling bad is ok and getting in the habit of not judging yourself -due to comparing yourself to others- for feeling how you feel will help you move on, let go, process the emotion and keep progressing towards what you want to do.

It was after the processing, non judgemental, letting go of the negative outcome that helped me dust myself down and start reapplying for magazines. What was different was I actually started to spend more time on them -taking them more seriously- and make sure that I adjusted and made sure the articles were the best I could write at the time. It was because of the negative feedback that I'm now a better writer and likely the reason you're holding this book in your hand today.

## *WINNING THE YOUNG ENTREPRENEUR OF THE YEAR AWARD*

This is a story of one of the biggest validation moments of my life. The day I didn't just get validation from my friends and family, but from strangers; I had the profound realisation that my story -just me being myself- was a story worth sharing and that others get a lot of value from it. The funniest thing about this was that It wasn't something I actively committed myself to. What you might not expect is that someone else put me forward for the "Young Entrepreneur Of The Year" award; I didn't actually put myself forwards.

I woke up one morning, a day just like any other, did my treatments, medicines and went to the gym just like any other day would start. Then I get an email, "thank you for applying for young entrepreneur of the year," and I freeze! "I didn't do that!" I thought, "Who did that!?" Then my mind went down the rabbit hole of thinking, "is this a joke or a scam?" -which I naturally did with any email I didn't want or ask for- My first thought was that It was a joke.

Then I got a message on social media from one of my friends, "have you checked your emails yet?" and I knew straight away that it was her that put me forward for this award. I instantly get defensive and ask her why she did it? I think my exact message went something like, "Why the hell would you put me forward for an award!?" or something like that.

To which she replied, "Why not? Your story is inspirational to a lot of people -you inspire me everyday- and you never know, maybe this is exactly what you need."

I had no idea what I was doing, I had to somehow get to Wales which is where the awards ceremony was being held and I also needed a suit -I hadn't worn a "dress suit" with a bow tie before- to that would be quite the experience to dress up like the penguin from batman. But all that was only if I got shortlisted and was invited to the event; which at the time I had done a good job of convincing myself that I wasn't going to be shortlisted and I should think nothing of it. At this point the whole experience with writing articles for magazines allowed me to notice that I was going down the emotional roller coaster again and I had to "get a handle on it" before it got too much. My self talk went from, "you'll never get shortlisted -and even if you did- you'd never be able to get there -and why bother anyway- you'll never actually win. I also thought to myself that it might be better off if I didn't get shortlisted (you're probably chuckling to yourself reading this process again).

I had completely let go of the idea and just went about my business; tennis coaching, personal training, looking after my own health... just like any other week. It was a couple of weeks before I got the news that I was actually shortlisted for the award and I did in fact need to find a way of getting to the ceremony if I wanted to go. It was voluntary, and it took some convincing for me to go; my friend said that it was a big moment for you and that you might kick yourself if you didn't go. She was right. It was interesting to me at the time how regretting not doing it started to be more of a pull than my fear of not winning the award; I thought, "well, there's only one winner and yet everyone turns up even though they know that, so it's not about the winning it's about the experience of going to a black tie awards ceremony."

So I got to work, needed to organise travel, hotel, suit and when I told my parents, my mother instantly said that she wanted to help me organise everything and go to the event with me for morale support. It might be weird but It actually made me feel more nervous because she was going -for some reason knowing no one knew me at the event made me feel a little more at ease- and yet also a little relieved because at least I would know someone at the event. But we organised everything and we were both ready to go (penguin suit and all).

A couple days before I made sure I had everything ready to go and suitcases were packed; I was extremely nervous and I just wanted to make sure at least I didn't forget anything. So I packed early, had the tickets and little bits of paperwork for the hotel easy to find so I didn't have to end up worrying or losing anything. Then the voices started, "What if I don't win? What if I did? What if I do the wrong thing? What if I say the wrong thing? Do I need to give a speech or not?" were just some of the things that were running through my mind because I'd never been to a black tie event, let alone an awards ceremony. Safe to say that I was coming up with anything to help me feel a little bit better and the more prepared I was, the better I seemed to feel. I told myself, "It'll be fine even if you don't win, You won't need to give a speech and it's only a little event."

On the day it wasn't as bad as I thought it would be because my mother offered to take me to the event, so it was a case of packing the car and off we went; we left with plenty of time and even had the chance to check out some of the local sights before we then started to get ready for the event. The nerves didn't really hit me as much until I started to get ready for the event.

While I was getting ready I was telling myself to just enjoy it, I probably wouldn't win the awards anyway and I should just be grateful that I was even shortlisted. There was a part of me that was so happy that I was even considered but I'm actually fairly competitive so deep down I did want to win too. I had to be on with that balancing act of being ok with not winning while secretly wanting to win. All this was going on while I was putting on my suit and my mother was getting ready too. I actually found that if I managed that emotional balancing act that I could keep control of my emotions and not "lose it" before I even got to the room the event was being held.

Luckily we were staying at the same hotel the event was being held at -which made things a lot easier for me- and I was able to not worry so much about being on time. That being said, as soon as I went downstairs and walked through the door of the awards ceremony I instantly felt "out of place" and awkward. It was like I hit a wall and I went from calm -ready to enjoy the night- to worrying about being judged negatively and I instantly felt myself tighten up; my back stiffened and I could feel my walk change from longer relaxed strides to shorter, almost shuffles. Luckily I was with my mother so we walked in, found a place to sit down and quickly sat down so I could take the weight off my feet and relax into the seat. As soon as I did that I felt a lot of relief and all the tension in my body seemed to disappear.

I was just glad I'd sat down because my legs kept saying to me that I'm only getting out of my seat for food, the toilet or if I win the award; I didn't want to get out of my seat unless I absolutely had to. Luckily there were plenty of others that seemed to stick to their seat too so I didn't look out of place and I tried to break the ice with some of the other people that were on my table, after convincing myself to have a good time that is. I'd start by asking the typical business questions like, "what do you do? How long have you been in business?" but then we suddenly got into curious questions like if they were a bakery I would ask them if they had anything they enjoyed baking the most like something they would take their time on. It passed the time before the event got into full swing.

The category I was nominated for was Young Entrepreneur Of The Year which was after a few categories; which was good so I could actually see how it works, if I needed to give any kind of speech and just see how the whole thing worked. I was really, really glad my category wasn't first. While they were introducing the guest speaker and going through the categories, my head started to play a weird game with me where it would spend the whole time convincing me that I wouldn't win, that I wasn't any good, worth winning the award and that I should just accept it. I mean I didn't know exactly what my friend told them so I started to feel like I should just enjoy the food, the company and feel really happy for those that were winning. So I did. I clapped for everyone and would pass a comment about how interesting or cool the winners were -as they mentioned a little about their business and why they won each time. I got to the point where I didn't care if I won or lost and that I was going to try to enjoy myself regardless.

Then Young Entrepreneur Of The Year was being announced and that suddenly changed; I looked over at my mother who was probably the only person in the room that was more nervous than me. With my heart pounding out of my chest, I felt like I was sweating everywhere -it's a good job I was wearing black- and all I could hear was the guest reading out the nominations... I felt time freeze when she read out my name and the snippet of my story of having health conditions while running a successful coaching business. I started to replay the conversation with myself around it not being important if I didn't win; telling myself it was just an award, that it didn't really mean anything.

There was a pause after the nominations were read out... "and the winner is...."

"..... Michael McDonnell!"

Everything froze, I was in complete shock, my heart sank and for a split second I wasn't really sure what to do. Do I get up? Or not? What the heck do I do? Time stood still and I glanced over at my mother who was in shock too. She started to cry with pride as I jumped up -I had to get out of my seat and collect this award I just won- so I power walked down the middle of the room, claps erupting as if I was walking out of a football stadium, my smile slowly getting bigger and bigger as I realised what I'd done and what was happening. I shook the presenter's hand, was given the award and stood for pictures before sitting back down again… Nothing ran through my mind other than "I bloody did it!!" I couldn't seem to get rid of this constant smile.

Suddenly everyone wanted to talk to me, have pictures with me, and someone even wanted to interview me about my business and the fact I won Young Entrepreneur Of The Year! It felt awkward but I also felt "at home" and weirdly enjoyed the attention. It was interesting how I enjoyed it when people came to me and wanted to know more about my business without me having to be all "extroverted" and make conversations with strangers; they came to me.

When I got back to the hotel room, I was still on a high of officially being an award winning entrepreneur and coach. It took me ages to sleep, but when I did I crashed out and ended up sleeping through my alarm -like the adrenalin completely knocked me out- but eventually we got packed, in the car and we drove back home. On the way back I realised that I got this massive boost in confidence.

Me "doing my thing" while having the conditions was enough to inspire others to do the same; to go after their goals no matter what. It felt extra weird as it all happened to me as such and at the time I didn't feel like I'd worked exceptionally hard for it; but that's because it was normal for me -but not others- and it took me a while to accept that. Recognition and acknowledgement of how far I'd come made it feel worth it to me, like I was on the right path and that I owe it to myself -and the people that use me for accountability, inspiration or motivation- to keep chasing my own dreams and goals. Almost like it gave me the permission to live in a way that gives others permission to do the same.

That's what winning the award meant to me because a couple of days later, things went back to normal for me. Aside from having this confidence and newfound belief in myself -and everyone seeming to respect me a little more- things simply went back to "normal" from my perspective pretty quickly. So because it was just one night, I had to then understand what this meant for my future; I understood that this was the permission I needed to do things I never thought I could, and that this was going to be the foundation that I would use to motivate me to make my life worth it.

## BEING INTERVIEWED ON SKY TV

It took around six to eight months for something else to come up for me; in the meantime I experienced a huge boost in how I felt about myself which meant I started to embrace and "own" the idea of me being an expert in my chosen field. It was a combination of me feeling confident and actually doing the things that experts in their field do.

At the time, I had built up the idea in my own mind that experts share their expertise; experts got published articles in magazines -I had another article featured before this- and were getting positive feedback and getting results from their content. I realised that things like this don't just happen -It might happen once you get noticed on a massive scale- but I had to go out there and create mine at the time. I had to write the articles, I had to put myself forward for interviews which I started to get.

I embraced the idea that I had to be proactive, I had to do the work if I was ever going to be seen as a trusted expert. Something else happened after that which caused me to practice what I preached and was an even bigger challenge for me than the articles and winning the award combined; I was interviewed on a TV show that aired on SKY about my journey of personal training and growing an online coaching business despite my health conditions. Despite the previous experiences giving me a sense of validation that I can share my story and be valuable to people, I still had a hard time accepting that they wanted to talk to me.

I was becoming more aware that I was simply going through the same process as the other times; so I was prepared for what I was about to go through emotionally, but I still had to be in a position where I could actually go through with the interview.

"I thought it would be cool" was my answer to myself about being on TV; it was always a bit of a pipe dream for me, I never thought I'd ever get the chance so it would never go on the goal boards or anything like that. I just never would have thought it would happen for me.

A friend stumbled on the show and website and told me to put myself forwards for the show; it was a mental health show and it played a huge part in my journey -after my previous experiences I had less self talk around applying for things as I got yes's and no's since- so I applied and completely let go of the idea that I'd get the yes. To tell you the truth I forgot about it. I accepted it would be a no and that I'd never hear from them again while carrying on with my personal training, tennis coaching and online business.

To put a time on this, I was running the tennis and personal training businesses part time -I had reduced my hours on purpose- to allow myself a little more "me time" and keep myself healthy. Then one day -I think it was a few months after I initially applied- I got an email I didn't expect and made me freak out! I got an email from the studio saying yes they would love for me to be a guest on the show... I didn't expect it!

I was almost in shock which made me worry a lot.....

My first worry was about how I would actually get there; I lived near Liverpool in the UK and the interview was in London -nearly five to six hours away- and I'd only ever been to London once before. Everything from where would I stay and then getting to the studio from the hotel was flying around my head -essentially more questions than answers- which caused something as simple as logistics of booking hotels overwhelming me. My mother wanted to come with me for morale support and so she could see me in action -I think she wanted to make sure I was safe too- and we eventually found the hotel I would book which luckily was only a short walk from the studio.

Once I had the date set and the accommodation booked, I started to worry and get anxious about other things; "What if I say the wrong thing?" Was the first thing that came up -almost immediately after booking the hotel- and I had a hard time overcoming this. I had started to convince myself that I wasn't good enough to handle the interview. Somehow -even after I'd been interviewed before- that I had convinced myself that this interview was different because it was on tv; telling myself things like, "a lot of people could be watching this, you need to be good" and starting to feel bad because I didn't feel I could do this.

When I thought about it, I had the thought of not being able to live up to the expectations and I felt this pressure around needing to be good. I felt like after sharing my story that I had built myself up to a level whereby they would be underwhelmed when they met me. Having health conditions and still being able to be an entrepreneur, coach and not conform to the labels or expectations that others put on me sounds like an inspirational story; and meeting me and realising that I'm "normal" felt like I wasn't actually successful and that I should be further along before being interviewed for tv.

What I was telling myself was centered around not being good enough again and what if they don't like me; and all of this was months before the interview and was giving myself a hard time. I noticed that I was jumping ahead to the interview -which I chuckled at and tried to not beat myself up about at the same time- as I thought I'd got to a point where I thought I was making progress on this personal development journey.

How can after all the work I've done on myself and how much I've managed to get through, why am I still just repeating the same cycle over and over again?

Is personal development pointless and a waste of time?

How can I possibly justify "doing the work on myself" when I still freak out when I have the opportunity to play at a bigger level?

These were just some of the things I started to tell myself when I hit my low point around the interview; I wasn't just beating myself up for being nervous despite having overcome my worries and fears before, but I was also beating myself up for having worked so hard on my mindset and mental health, and it all came crashing down because I was doing something scary for the first time again. I felt like I had wasted my time and started to question whether "mindset work" was even helpful.

This lingered around for around one to two days before I started to tell myself something different.

One of the first things I did was tell myself that I was better than this and to pull myself together. I had to give myself a bit of a "telling off" because assuming that just because I had been on this personal development journey doesn't make me invincible -I'm human, just like you reading this- and I had to accept that I was going to inevitably feel anxious or negative sometimes and I had to deal with it as and when it showed up.

I had to gradually understand that the fact they said yes was proof that I was good enough; that I could handle it and that I was a good fit for the show. I spent a long time talking myself down and convincing myself that I wasn't good enough, searching for the validation and permission that I'd needed.... And it was staring me in the face.

A week before the big day I was rehearsing my answers to potential questions; I had no idea what she would ask but I felt I needed something to occupy my mental space otherwise I'd go down a negative "hole" again. I only really did this to help calm my nerves as I thought that the more I'd prepare for the interview, the better I would feel. I also started doing certain things when I felt nervous like walks, breathing exercises or simply meditating for ten minutes. When I noticed the nerves "bubbling up" I would do what I could before they got to a point I couldn't manage them. Which got harder the closer I got to the day.

This is it -the day of the interview- and I'm a complete bag of nerves! I barely slept, felt "groggy," shaking, like I'd gone ten rounds with Mike Tyson and all I could think about was the interview. "Oh my god, oh my god, oh my god, oh my god....." became my inner voice and there wasn't much I could do that would shut that off. I found that I was struggling to eat and I'd forget little things that I would otherwise easily remember to do. Slowly, the thought of being on sky tv was all I could think about.

If I had any chance of being calm, collected and grounded for the interview, I had to manage my energy levels which meant forcing myself to eat, go the gym and look after myself; luckily I had packed the day before so I didn't have to worry about that -it helped me feel more in control- and I could focus on mentally and physically preparing for the interview.

On my way to London and -as I got closer and closer- I could feel my heart pounding out of my chest, dehydrated because of how much I was sweating -I had to keep drinking to keep up- and I felt like I couldn't relax until I got to the hotel. I would walk up and down the platform trying not to think about what I was doing, distracting myself with anything I could. Luckily we had plenty of time for unpacking and food -as we picked the hotel that was close to the studio- and we spent the majority of the time relaxing, eating, and chatting to take my mind off later on.

This was it -now was the time- I was all ready to go! I made sure I was early -slowly walking towards what I thought was the studio- and I went in, shaking, trying to put on a brave face. First I was in the green room and there were others being interviewed, refreshments were available but I didn't feel like eating. I just wanted to get it over and done with, get through it. Soon it would be my turn and someone came out to greet us and talk us through what was going to happen -I listened because I had no idea what I was doing or what to expect- but I ended unjust focusing on the fact that I'm actually there, actually being interviewed for sky and that I was actually doing this.

Heavy legs started, nervous stomach, couldn't think straight and my breathing was getting shallower and quicker; and as I walked through the green door onto the studio there was a part of me that wanted to run away; I slowly creeped towards the chair that was clearly meant for me -greeting the camera crew while I made my way to the seat- and felt myself sink into the seat when I sat down. I started a quick conversation with the host to help break the ice and help me settle in -all I could think about were the cameras, the lights and just how anxious I was- but all that did help. She was really welcoming and helpful so I just had to get through it. Lights, camera, action!

As soon as we started I felt the pressure disappear and I just spoke -like a weight had been lifted- which felt weird at first; eventually it gave me the space I needed to speak without thinking too much about what I was saying. I kept thinking "slow down" so I could take my time and simply give my best answers to the hosts questions. Sometimes I'd notice myself talking too fast as I was nervous; but I did it. I was so relieved after the interview that I felt my toes relax -It felt like I was on a roller coaster- but I also enjoyed it too. It was a strange combination of stress, nerves, enjoyment and relief after the whole thing was over, "I enjoyed it but I'm glad it's over!"

After the interview, me and my mother went out for something to eat, she said how good she thought I did and how proud of me she was that I did it. I wasn't sure I agreed but we ate, talked, relaxed and first thing tomorrow we went back home.

## *LESSONS FROM MICHAEL*

After all these things, I felt myself being very reflective around why I was going them -what was the point- and I thought that sometimes seeking validation and permission can be a good thing because no one knows -in the initial stages anyway- if they're capable of putting themselves out there -if they can handle it- so sometimes it's good to have someone else to open the door and tell you you're ready. Them saying yes is the validation and permission.

Another thing I thought about was that telling myself anything positive -even if I didn't know it was true- still helped me. As stupid and crazy as it sounds, if there's no real proof for either -good or bad- you have to ask yourself what conversation woul you rather have with yourself? You can tell from my experiences at this point involved me changing the conversation in my own head for me to be able to do what I did; do you think I could have been on tv without that? Maybe, but I can tell you that it would be much harder for me to actually follow through with them and I could have stopped or gave up.

The knock backs and the cycle of sending articles got me thinking that eventually, the negative moments simply don't last as long anymore because of the work I did on myself. What I realised was that I bounced back much quicker the more you go through it and I found myself more aware of what was happening while it was happening. That allowed me to "catch" the negativity early before it took over my thoughts so I could keep myself acting from a more positive space than I otherwise would. That's the big thing, it's not about completely removing fear, anxiety or negative thinking; it's about how long you spend positive versus negative and shifting it in your favour as often as possible. Looking back. judging myself for feeling bad or not being superhuman didn't help and personal development is a continuous process and something you have to do everyday which I had to embrace and understand.

What I didn't realise at the time was that It's ok to do things that reduce your nerves or negative feelings. Doing whatever it takes to practically handle the situations you're in isn't anything to be ashamed of or guilty about because you don't see others doing it. You don't know what's going on behind the scenes of the majority of speakers or public figures -It's perfectly normal and natural to feel nervous or afraid sometimes- so if you have to have practices or procedures in place so you can get through it... then so be it.

## This Changed My Life Forever

Before you can really understand how being diagnosed with diabetes completely changed the direction of my life, gave me the mortality motivation I needed to commit fully to that direction, and experience the questions you ask yourself when you think you're near the end; you need to know the full story. I always went after what I enjoyed, what I wanted, or what I was good at. It made sense to me that I would do that versus just do what I was given; I liked the idea of creating it but this would be the moment that lights the fire underneath me that lasts years to come.

As you know, I was always into fitness from as early as I can remember, in my earlier years it was martial arts and football that got me into the idea of keeping active (I guess initially for health reasons) before I moved on to basketball, tennis and then I found working out when I was fifteen thanks to my uncle. To say I was a health nut when it came up exercising would be an understatement. When I became a personal trainer and group exercise instructor, I took things to a whole new level; I'd exercise multiple times a day, I'd go for walks and when CrossFit exploded I jumped on the bandwagon of, "work on your weaknesses" and mixing disciplines like weightlifting, gymnastics and cardiovascular exercise to get myself into the best shape of my life!

At that time, I was even focused on my diet; I had to eat a lot as I was so active but I would make adjustments and always attempt the healthier options.

## *MY FRIEND*

When you have cystic fibrosis, there's a term called "crossinfection" which means that if people with cystic fibrosis spend too long together, we can infect each other and make eachother worse. It's because of that, that there aren't any support groups or meet ups and that we meet doctors and nurses with limited contact with other patents to minimise the likelihood of getting unwell or ending up struggling just because we mingle with others with similar conditions.

With all that's going on, and with the way hospitals organise themselves, families have a better chance of meeting each other and getting to know each other than the patients do; and they did. Over time, our family got close to another family, for as long as I could remember. We seemed to either cross paths or parents would meet in the cafe to chat while we were at appointments. Their son, who was only a year older than me, (let's call him Dave) had cystic fibrosis and diabetes which impacted him a lot more than just cystic fibrosis. Extra treatments and specialists in order to manage the extra contraindication.

We started to get on, Dave and I, we realised we could only really talk between meetings and rarely could actually sit and chat, but it was likely the best relationship we could have with someone with the same conditions.

Things went to the next level -so to speak- one year when we ended up playing in the same 5-a-side football team; we met up for the training sessions and matches just like any other team. At first it was weird seeing someone that I would only see at hospital, out in the real world, but I eventually got used to it. We played matches, laughed, and it started to feel like I had a friend that also knew about "behind the scenes." Something I never thought I'd have. I always remember the time when we were playing an away match -that we lost if I remember right- but we still celebrated as a team because of how well we played.

It hit me harder than I thought it would, the moment I found out he passed away. I had lost friends before but this was different, I wasn't old enough to really understand what was going on; but this time I did. I was angry, I felt like there must be something I could have done to help or just anything that would mean he was still alive. I took my anger out on as few people as I could -failed sometimes- and spent longer in the gym over the next few days to weeks taking my frustrations out there. It made me realise that anything could happen, your time can end at any time and that the conditions don't discriminate; they can take you at any moment.

After a few weeks of wallowing, processing and deciding to take a couple of things more seriously in my own life health wise, I did start to feel better. I was exercising almost everyday to take my frustrations out, but I also felt like I needed to shift why I exercised. Over the years I've exercised to look better, to feel better, to be stronger and fitter than ever -and I do still do that- but I felt like I needed to be more conscious of my overall health and not sacrifice that just to be a little stronger or feel a little fitter that week. Losing Dave shifted me towards longevity and factoring in how I could benefit years from now, not just in the short or medium term.

I took that mentality with me into other areas of my life too -which I'll go into detail on further into the chapter-... it was time to make a huge change. I was a personal trainer and tennis coach at the time so keeping fit and healthy was an important part of my business and my life. But I had no idea just how much of a shift and change I would make, what happened after that changed everything for me and altered the course of my life.

## *I THOUGHT IT WAS JUST LIKE ANY OLD HOSPITAL APPOINTMENT*

On a typical day like any other, every two months I'd go into the hospital for my usual check up; checking in to see how I'm doing and making sure cystic fibrosis was being kept at bay. I'd go through a series of tests and they'd always compare it to last time and likely a couple appointments further back to check the trend. I always tended to do well and it was always a case of "see you next time." I thought this would be like any other appointment.... But it wasn't.

Once you get to a certain age with cystic fibrosis, you're susceptible to being diabetic. A quick run down of the types: type one is the organ -your pancreas- doesn't function optimally so needs help, type two is diet related as fat -and likely other things- build up around the outside of the pancreas causing insulin to struggle to be released in your blood, cystic fibrosis related diabetes -CFRD- involves "mucus" building up on the inside stopping insulin from being released. CF is where your body produces excessive mucus anyway so this can happen over time. I was in the age category so the nurses wanted to run a test over three to five days just to see if I was diabetic.

I thought nothing of it, "I can't be diabetic!" I thought so I just agreed. I put a continuous glucose monitor on my arm and kept track of my exercise and diet for five days; I went to the gym with it on, I ate my normal meals and just did my usual routines. After the five days I sent it back to them to look at and I didn't think any more of it until I went back for my next appointment.

Again, as if everything was normal, I'd wake up, take my inhalers, nebulisers, medicines and do my physiotherapy; just like I would normally do. I drove to the hospital and went through my usual routine, sat down in front of the nurse who had my crumpled up food and exercise diary in front of her, and with a clinical unemotional voice said, "according to the data and the food you ate, I'm sorry to say you're diabetic; now while it's a common thing for adults with CF to also have diabetes, it does mean a lifestyle adjustment and also injecting insulin everyday."

I felt like the floor disappeared from underneath me, time stopped for me, I froze. I'd worked so hard all my life on my health, from when I was younger until now, I'd spent countless hours, became someone that helps others with their health and fitness, only to be told I have one of the worst health related conditions. I felt like all the years were for nothing, everything I'd done was pointless and It's like I needed to do more, not less, in a world where I felt like I couldn't do much more. I felt broken.

But here's what's worse, here's the thinking that really hit me like a ton of bricks; my mind instantly thought to my friend, Dave, who passed away with these conditions and I thought that I was next, that I couldn't stop this thing from taking me too and that I was powerless to stop this thing. Dave was only a year older than me and the mortality rate for people with CFRD wasn't far behind Dave or me. What was I going to do?

I felt like this was it, I was done, I started shaking, sweating, trying not to cry, sat in front of the nurse and no matter what she said, no matter how much she tried to make it feel not such a bad thing; I couldn't even hear her. I zoned out, all I could think about was, "why me? Have I lived how I wanted to live? Have I done right by me and the people I loved? If I'd lived a life I would be proud of... did I matter?"

Something that I'm actually not wanting to write, but I will anyway, is that I genuinely wasn't sure If I wanted to go on anymore....

The answers my mind went to were not promising, didn't fill me with joy or any sense of relief at all. I tried to deny it, I asked for a retest and I would adjust my diet to see if I could simply adjust what I was eating, they agreed. So I went through the whole process again, I cut out as many carbs as I could within reason -I needed to eat after all- and the test again came back the same. I was given my monitors, told what insulin I was to start taking and when, and that was it. My life had officially changed forever; not because of the diagnosis, but what the diagnosis meant for me.

I had to focus on my health even more -as if it wasn't enough already- and the balancing act officially started around sugar, carbs, other foods, stress levels, exercise. Everything became even more delicate than it already was, along with the mental impact of now having the conditions that Dave had. I honestly couldn't believe it. I realized that the answers to my questions actually made me feel horrible because It wasn;t enough, I wanted more.... I wanted to have way better answers to those questions: did I do right by me and the people

I love? Do the people I love know it? Do I show it often? Did I matter? Would I be remembered?

I answered no to pretty much all of them, and it made me feel terrible; it made me feel like I didn't amount to anything even after the years of doing what I thought was right. It made me feel like I'd end up doomed to go through the motions or be confined because of my -now- two conditions. I went through a phase of hating the world, hating myself, not because of what happened (that's what you're probably thinking) but because I couldn't do anything about it, I couldn't change it. I felt so disempowered and that I had to "let it happen" to a certain extent… which I hated.

Then and there -in the hospital- I decided to play bigger; before I even left the building I made the decision to start my online business and change more lives. I'd keep the tennis coaching and personal training as long as I could, but ultimately I had to prioritise impacting more people with my message and that became the filter for my decisions. It made things easier eventually but there was a log of "growing pains" when I looked into the online business world as there was far too much information out there. This was the start, this was ground zero for everything you see me do today.

**_DO YOU HAVE A FILTER FOR YOUR DECISIONS?_**

One of the things that hit me was the fact that I would start to do things that would allow me to touch more lives in a positive way. I went from going through the motions -sticking to what I was good at- to going full throttle into the unknown. But, I was doing it for a reason; I had a purpose behind it and that would cause me to think, speak and act intentionally towards it. Because I started asking myself completely different questions from what I was asking before, the answers changed with them. The word I used at the time was "filter" as they were questions I used to reduce my options and possibilities until you have a small enough amount of them to act on.

I went from asking myself, "what's next?" to. "What's possible?" which likely seems weird because they look like they're the same; but let me explain. What's next brings into light my past, where I am right now, and what the next steps are. What's possible doesn't really do that; it opens the door to possibilities, to avenues that may or may not factor in what came before. I was a tennis coach and personal trainer that had -now- two health conditions; factoring my past in was going to slow me down. When I asked myself questions like, "what's possible? What can I do? How can I impact more people?" opens the door to me being creative, me essentially drawing a line in the sand and starting something new, no limits, no restrictions, nothing and no one stopping me, aside from myself. Being possibility minded changed everything for me.

### "What would you do IF you don't factor in your past or your present?"

I understand that this could bring up a lot of fear for you, a lot of questions and worries around it. I've got bills to pay, I've got a family and responsibilities that rely on me; and I don't want you to stop doing the thing that covers that. What sort of person would I be to tell you to drop everything and go all in on a possibility when you have safety and responsibilities to consider; but what if you had an hour a day you could dedicate to the path that could change your entire life. You could spend an hour a day researching, learning, finding the elements of the thing you desperately want to do -the thing that keeps you up at night because you secretly regret not doing- and going for it.

Imagine the fulfilment and sense of happiness that you would feel if you could spend an hour a day towards the impact you want to make that isn't fulfilled with the way you fulfil your responsibilities as a human. It's possible, it's doable and actually fairly straightforward to find an hour a day or two blocks of thirty minutes.

I didn't start spending all day everyday on this, I started my "online thing" alongside being a personal trainer and tennis coach and I'd spend the spare time I had between clients, travel between venues, food, sleep, family, friends, my own training, my own tennis and other hobbies. As you can imagine, I was at the point where I found a way -which started off difficult- but over time it started to integrate into my life the idea of doing things for safety and responsibilities, then around that I'd find a way to work on my bigger online empire. I did what I could, until it started to take Its toll

## I HAD TO MAKE AN IMPORTANT DECISION

As soon as I started the "online thing" alongside my businesses I noticed something; I noticed that there was an entire planet on my phone where people spent their time... it was completely overwhelming! Between social media, email marketing, websites and more, I had to navigate this new world in my pocket.

I entered social media initially: Twitter, Facebook and Instagram were the first platforms I used. After reading blogs on how to use them, looking at how others used it too gave me the structure to follow which actually made me nervous. "Why did it make you nervous Mike?" I hear you ask; well it was because I saw the influencers posting multiple times a day per platform with Twitter being posting nearly every thirty minutes! Long story short, keeping up with social media became like a full time job for me and it suddenly got overwhelming and difficult at the same time.

Between the lack of self confidence, the struggling with self worth, and trying to learn the platforms at the same time as this being a lot of work and overwhelming me.... I slowly burned out.

The start of the spiral was that I was simply on edge all the time, which meant I struggled to sleep. I always remember the time when I would worry if I hadn't posted yet. Sat in the gym or the tennis club eating a snack between clients and id think, "oh no, I haven't posted yet!" and I'd freak out, grab my phone, and quickly come up with something to post, post it, then I felt the relief and I'd be able to breathe. Imagine that... but multiple times a day; along with the stress that comes with working with clients, looking after myself enough to be able to play tennis, be better than my clients, and being able to concentrate enough to give my tennis/fitness clients one hundred percent of my time and attention. This "constantly on" is something that I was completely new to, didn't expect and didn't plan or prepare for. If you can imagine the long term effects of this, not being able to switch off, then not really being able to sleep and recover from the day before; that was my life.

After realising that sleep was very important for me, this started the questions running through my head.

Am I prepared to sacrifice my health to be successful?

If things got any worse, can I handle it?

What's it going to take for me to make the mark I want to make, and will I actually be able to before my health gets too bad?

What if "as far as I'm prepared to go" and as far as I CAN go, are different?

What if I actually deteriorate beyond recovery before I get there?

As a result of that I started to feel generally more stressed out than normal, like everything was getting on top of me and the smallest thing would cause me to snap. Being late for things would wind me up and as soon as I noticed it I started to take steps. The first thing I did was I would force myself to go in the sauna and then the cold pool at the leisure center; it would sweat out the toxins (or that's what it felt like) and then the cold exposure would shock me into relaxing or relieving myself of some of what was eating at me. I'm sure there's science to back some of that up, but I'm simply sharing how it helped me. I needed to perform a few rounds of that -hot sauna, cold pool- until I felt the benefit; and it did, it started to feel amazing. Then I started to look into the benefits of music and I realised that if I listened to more upbeat music, I felt better; so I did that. Combine that with doing my best to meditate and get a massage every now and again; the stress side did start to not affect me as long as I actually dedicated time to reducing it in the diary. It needed to be in the diary otherwise it wouldn't happen.

The diary was an interesting thing because I had no real control over my schedule and I was at the point in my life where I had enough of struggling and I was willing to change everything to improve things; so the diary was next. I allocated a certain number of days for tennis, fitness, and specifically for the "online thing" so I could maybe be a little slower because I'd spend dedicated time on it. The tennis got easier, the fitness got a little easier and the online business got easier over time. I'm a big advocate for organising yourself makes a lot of things easier but I was getting to the point where I needed to schedule in time alone -time by myself- in order to manage everything.

Two lifestyle businesses, slowly showing up multiple times a day online while managing two health conditions was a giant balancing act with a spanner in the works; why? Because I had no idea what It was like to be diabetic, a fitness nut & tennis coach. I fought it, battled it for months, I thought I was tired but because of something else, maybe I had been working out too hard and just needed to factor in more stretches or "body maintenance" like yoga, walks ect but there was much more to it. I got to a point where I was going to burn out no matter what.

I started to then get restless in the night no matter what I tried, which meant that I couldn't fully recover from the day before; it was a spiral downwards. What made it worse was one of the only things I knew how to do, that gave me energy, was either eating sweets or drinking a lot of caffeine. I knew it wasn't right, I knew that It wouldn't help me long term and I was on this cycle of a lot of energy, then no energy, but I needed something and unfortunately my lack of knowledge around handling the "down moments" meant I did the best with what I had. I always remember the moment I had had enough; the moment I decided there and then that I needed a big change, not just little changes.

This was around the same time that my clients saw my story in a local magazine and I was also on local radio -being recognised for the first time because of that was very surreal- but this means that my story was out there for all to see and I started to share more because I had before. It was almost like once I had gotten over the hurdle of sharing for the first time, it started to get easier and easier to keep sharing it. What happened next was crazy!

They started to have the mindset of, "you can do all you can do with having these health conditions; and say I'm struggling -or can't lose weight- when I don't have anything 'wrong' with me... I don't have any excuses anymore." This caused my clients to get much more dramatic results. Weight loss, much fitter, healthier, happier, calmer... all because I had shared how difficult it could be for me because I started in a "lesser" position. They also shared how motivational and inspirational I am -which was very odd and slightly embarrassing at the time- and that I should share my story more; "I should put myself out there more as your story is very powerful" they would say to me. I became convinced that If I could help people with their health and fitness, I could help people in other areas too.

The entire string of events over the last say six to twelve months gave me the realization I needed to do a couple of things: get more serious with my online business, look for ways to become a public speaker and find a way to make it work. The more I shared my story, the more I shared my knowledge, the more entrepreneurs and business owners were drawn to me because I was one too. You see, because I lived it, was living it, and it was normal to me, I had never even considered that It was "enough" to me just being me. Me, the guy that always thought he was the worst in the room, the guy that spent most of his life avoiding the potential pain. I had no idea the impact It could have on others and the idea of transforming lives through my story alone hit me pretty hard because I couldn't wrap my head around it.

It simply challenged the way I saw the world, challenged my reality, and that's what made it so hard to accept. I would tell myself things like, "Noone wants to know that, that's not valuable, I'm not special, everyone knows this, surely it's common sense." I spent a long time downgrading myself, my story and what I've gone through in an attempt to fit in -blend in... like highschool- and be seen to be similar to the people I spent my time with. That was the thing, where I came from, so few actually made something of themselves outside of getting a job and that's it; that was the life. That was what was normal, so the very idea of being someone different to that wasn't even understood; nevermind accepted, allowed or celebrated. Breaking the mold was my natural state -being different was my entire life- and I went from seeing it as not this huge thing -to finally seeing it as a good thing- as a powerful thing and that I could start to do something with it. It was time I stood above the normal and made something of my difference.

Maybe this is something you, yourself, have experienced too? Maybe you simply can't wrap your head around something, so you discount it, you brush it off, you ignore it; but what if it's the one thing that can change everything for you?

Do you have anything that's "normal" or "easy" for you, and perhaps you haven't yet realised how valuable you can be to someone else? Have a think, think long and hard about it because you may have a gift that you can bring to the world; you may have something special that you think isn't special at all. This will take a lot of soul searching -not letting your opinion of yourself get in the way- writing out the things you think are easy, writing out your story and the principles of what makes your thing easy for you. You never know who might need exactly what's easy for you.

## **My Public Speaking Journey**

After a handful of conversations made me realise that my story was valuable, entertaining and inspirational, I made the decision to start the "online thing" and get into public speaking. I called it the online thing as it was new, I didn't know if it would work and I guess I started out casual with the idea initially. But it was the public speaking I wanted to do.

I got to work looking at different events to speak at -used no less than google to start with- and I found hundreds of events all around the world. I started to panic because I wasn't sure If I was prepared to fly to my first ever event; I didn't know if I was good enough at speaking or if it was something I really wanted to do. It took me a few weeks of looking online until I found an event within travel distance that I could try my hand at public speaking.

I'll admit, I was nervous, excited, and scared. I was scared because all the reasons I had for not doing this were solved. What if I wasn't good enough; well it wasn't a big event and it was an "open mic" event so anyone could speak. What if I run out of things to say or freeze on stage; the slot was only five minutes and you needed slides as part of the event... so if in doubt I could use the slides to fall back on. It's too far away; well actually I found one I could get to on the train or even drive to if I really wanted. It's a crazy feeling when you have all your excuses handled because you feel the fear rise up, you have all the excuses under the sun but you naturally try to solve them yourself... talk about realizing they were all excuses and reasons to not face something deep down you really wanted to do. Once you understand that sometimes your reasons for not doing something are your blueprint for making what you want happen, a lot can change for you, as they did for me. I found my event, I found my first shot at public speaking, and I decided to grab it with both hands.

The event was a few months away which gave me plenty of time to prepare....

That doesn't mean I wasn't nervous -I was- and I felt like I had made a mistake; I wondered if It was the right thing or if I would be better sticking to what I knew I was good at. It was only after I had this conversation, that I would actually convince myself not to cancel and to go through with it. I had to have answers to the questions my head would ask me otherwise this would be a very short experiment that would go badly. It'll be written as if it was a conversation with myself.

*So Mike, you fancy yourself a public speaker?*
I do, deep down I feel like I was called to do this; I always felt a little fed up with playing small and my personal training clients mentioning that my story was inspirational but also having practical elements too just confirmed the desire I have. They told me that it gave them permission to think differently

119

and act differently and that I should not let my story go unheard.

*You do realise you've never done this before?*
Yes, but everyone starts somewhere, thousands of hours on stage starts with the first one and I know I will get better the more I do it. Practice makes permanent and If I learn from it and improve on my mistakes each time, I'll get better the more I practice.

*What makes you think you can do this? Who are you to think you can be a public speaker?*
This question I actually had a hard time answering; because of my past I still felt this "I'm not good enough" feeling. The only way I was able to get around this was to accept that my ability to do this would likely be shown in feedback or the way the crowd responded to my talk. I could stay in my head around this for months and months never realising that I could do it because the crowd clapped, laughed or something similar. This was a case of "the results would speak for themselves" so I had to

get through it in order to find out if I was good enough.

*What if you mess it up? What if they laugh at you?*
I don't know the answer to this one; how would I know If I failed? If I felt like I failed, It would likely hit me for a couple of weeks. I'd have to likely take some time out to recover. But here's the thing, this would mean I had to still actually get through it. I would still have to get up on that stage and do my best before seeing how the audience would respond to it; and if they laughed at me because I messed up, it would be about how I responded after that. I'm trying to pre-predict what will happen -and make that true- which I realise I can only do if I don't make any effort at all. If I plan, practice, rehearse and do my best to not crumble mentally, the chances of things going horrible will obviously be slim.

But I'll do everything I can to make sure I don't mess up, I can only do my best and see what happens. Oh, and I would likely put it down to lack of experience if I did "fail" by my own definition, figure out how I could improve, then try again... because I want to do this and I'm prepared to fail on my way there.

*What if the whole thing would be for nothing? What if it's a waste of time?*
How would I know? Much like the previous question, there's an element of trying to get too far ahead of myself and then prevent the negative form happening by not acting; which was something I spent all my younger years doing, so I got very good at it. Remember, Mike, don't let avoiding negativity stop you from moving towards what you want.

After having this conversation I got to work, I thought that if I started recording videos, that would help. I started recording standing videos, got myself a tripod and recorded multiple times a week, then everyday once I got more comfortable. I wasn't a fan of how I sounded so I didn't watch them back; I couldn't change my voice and I wanted to prevent myself from getting too obsessed with it. I set the bar so low for the videos -turn on the camera and talk- that It allowed me to be consistent, didn't judge myself, didn't hate myself, which gave me the chance to improve over time. It wasn't easy, I went from very self conscious, almost like time slowed right down because of how nervous I was, to just being able to turn on the camera and talk without being hyper aware. The more I did it, the better I became.

After doing some research on the event, I realised that they were timed talks with slides; so there would be a set start, end and each slide would be shown for a set amount of time. I got to work on the slides, worked on my timings in the weeks leading up to the event day which gave me a sense of, "if I stick to the timings and do my best to do as rehearsed, it makes it easier to just get through it." It helped me reduce the bar for getting through it, which was the minimum for me. "Just get through it" was something I told myself from around two weeks before the day of the event while I was preparing, planning, rehearsing, at the same time as running my tennis coaching, personal training and the "online thing."

## ON THE DAY

The talk was in the evening but I couldn't stop thinking about it from the week before, the day before, and the entire day up until after I got through it. I was nervous, bags of energy, I couldn't get the talk out of my head and "the voices" were louder than ever. It was like the closer I got to the time, the louder they got until they started to just be "aaaaahhhhh" on repeat in my head. If you ever think that it gets easier when you're moving towards your dreams -doing things that scare you- then you would be wrong. The thought of doing it was bad enough; but actually taking the steps, actually making progress and doing the thing is way scarier and it took a lot for me to actually get on the stage. Let me talk you through it.

From when I woke up, my only focus was preparing myself for being on stage that evening. I did as much as I could to make sure I was in the best possible place for the talk. I made sure I went to bed early the night before, and got plenty of sleep. I'd go through my usual morning routine -medicines, physio, treatments- with a couple of changes; I would listen to podcasts but also a music playlist I'd put together of my favourite uplifting songs -this playlist I would play almost on loop the entire day- and I drank around a liter of water.

After that I got myself ready for my usual gym session, which was also different as I focused on stretching and relaxing alongside my usual morning spinning class; which I also did at around sixty percent of my usual effort level as I didn't want to wear myself out for the evening. Stretches for my whole body, I'd spend some time just lying down focusing on my breathing to help calm my nerves between stretches; it felt like a full on meditation session with myself but drinking water throughout. After that, I showered -hot and cold exposure shower- and got ready to attack my day.

I thought it's worth mentioning that this was conveniently a day where I wasn't working, I moved my tennis and fitness clients and it just so happened to be a day where I didn't have any obligations to either business... but I did still show up online with posts, pictures and videos. This was one of the keys for me as I could focus on preparing myself. I was a mess, so I tried to give myself the day to look after myself without distractions.

So I got back, and It was running an online business, to make sure I eat enough and keep my energy high. I bought plenty of food beforehand so it was as easy as preparing them and eating them. Prepreparing things seemed to go well so far.

I lived with my parents so after I ate I did my usual thing which was walking with my mother to work, then walking to my local park -which was around twenty minutes- where I would record videos, check in with clients, write my posts for the day and organise my content for the day. It was convenient that my walk to and from the park was when I would get as much work done as possible to help fill the mental space and make the most of my time. I kept a bottle of water with me the whole time -constantly sipping- so I could keep myself well hydrated. At this point I found a cafe, got myself a cup of tea, and sat with the talk slides on my phone and ran through them over and over again. A couple of hours would go by, I'd order another tea and something to eat -I think it was a sandwich and a small chocolate cake- and sit memorising what I'd say, how long each slide would take to make sure I had all the information I needed in my head.

After that I sat and organised travel; I felt that getting the train would avoid more problems than driving like traffic and finding somewhere to park. It was more convenient and less stressful than driving myself; luckily I was a walk away from the train station so I could get there fairly easily and then essentially be driven to Liverpool, UK, which was where the talk was. Also, because I didn't have to focus on driving, I could focus on relaxing, calming my nerves, going over the presentation and listening to my positive music playlist.

Fast forward through eating, posting online and answering clients; walking to the train station, listening to podcasts and music, telling myself things like, "you'll be ok, you'll be fine, you can do this." luckily the walk helped to clear my mind and I was able to just about keep the negative voices at bay. At least for now. One of the things I made sure I did was to be early; the timing of the event meant that I could be on time but eat before I set off, or eat in Liverpool and be a couple of hours early. As you can probably guess, I opted for being early as that would alleviate some of the stress or pressure.

When I got off the train, things started to change for me; the stories I told myself before I decided to challenge myself as a public speaker started to resurface. I started to question myself all over again. Question whether I should do this, whether I was good enough, whether I was ready... I felt the shift in my head and -if im being completely honest- I didn't prepare for...... as I got closer it got louder and louder, I had to slow down my walking so I could focus, I felt my anxiety skyrocket so I had to slow my breathing down

Eventually I arrived -hours early- so I had plenty of time to soak up the nerves, get used to the environment and at least begin to feel comfortable; as you can imagine, it took me a while just for the voices to calm down, but they eventually did as I got to where I needed to be. Almost like the need to be somewhere went away which helped calm me down. Because I was diabetic I needed to keep myself awake and not crash before my talk; it felt weird to time when to eat but as the talk was at about eight oclock in the evening, it felt appropriate as id still need to get home afterwards -I didn't want to crash on the way home either- so I had to do what I had to do. A combination of teas, hot chocolates with marshmallows and a sandwich was enough for me to feel like I had the energy to make it to the train on the way back easily. It was time to get ready to "face the music" and experience what It was like to be on stage for the first time.

## *AT THE EVENT*

My talk was on lifestyle design, but I was about the fourth speaker into the event; this meant I could see a few of the other speakers and see how it all worked as it was my first time. What I didn't realise -of course- was that I would instantly compare myself to them and decide that my talk wouldn't be as good as theirs. That happened almost straight away and filled me with dread for my own talk. I could feel the sweat slowly dripping down my back and my hands got all sweaty while I was watching the other speakers, "they're all doing so well, I can't do this." What made things worse was one of the speakers I found the courage to speak to was a university professor! He spoke and gave lectures pretty much everyday; PHDs, TEDx speakers... and me. I felt completely out of place. I just wanted to curl up in the corner and hide; but I was about to do something that I never thought I could and curling up and hiding was the opposite of what I needed to do. Isn't it odd that what the situation demanded from me was exactly the opposite of what I wanted to do?

As the speakers went on, did their thing, and was applauded off, it got closer and closer to the moment when I would be called out. My heart was racing at this point, I had been to the toilet just to walk around, and a nervous stomach meant I was back and to quite a bit. With my entire body on fire, shaking in my seat, and my hands shivering too -I needed a drink just so I could hold onto something and stop my hands shaking- ... I was about to be introduced.

When the host said my name it was like time froze, I froze, "this was it" I thought. My legs didn't want to move and I felt like a statue for what felt like forever; but it was only for a couple of seconds. I stood up, slowly walking to the stairs, trying to smile while having to convince myself to pick my feet up one by one and put them down one in front of the other. Walking became something I had to tell myself was a good idea and every fiber of me didn't want to go up there -in front of around a hundred people- and give the talk I was rehearsing for a week before. I felt like I couldn't breathe, couldn't think anything except "don't do it, you'll do so badly, they'll laugh, they'll hate you." All I could think was, "oh my god, oh my god, oh my god, this is it, this is your moment, breathe, breathe mike, relax, one foot in front of the other... that's it, you're doing it!" That was on repeat from seat to stage; along with mentally rehearsing the presentation, slowly walking with heavy legs and sweaty palms, and trying to slow my mile a minute heart from racing. I could feel the carpet sink under my feet with every step I took up the stairs to the stage; it felt like it took a lifetime to get up on stage, but I made it.

Aside from hearing my heartbeat, feeling the sweat flowing down my back and hands and shouting at myself to speak, to say something, I don't remember much about my talk at all. The only things I remember were my standards increasing as soon as I got over the "just get up there and talk"… I wanted to do a good job…It was like I went from the bare minimum to "it needs to be good mike" within about three seconds. Once I had got over the hurdle of getting on the stage, that was it. A short break in my freaking out when the audience laughed at something I said. My body and mind was operating at such a high rate that the only thing I was focused on was the fact that everyone was staring at me, I was very hot, sweating, and I felt like everything I was doing or saying was either wrong, freaky or not good enough. It felt like five minutes of hell, I felt every millisecond but don't completely remember it.

## *AFTERWARDS*

After the talk was finally over I walked off the stage, bounced down the stairs like a child, sat down on my chair as if I was sitting on a beanbag after a very long day at work. Breathed a sigh of relief and then I slowly felt the thoughts slow down enough to be able to understand them; "OMG I did it, I actually did it." I felt my arms and legs flop down like a rag doll after an hour long massage; I felt this sense of whole body relaxation, like the stress, pressure and "weight" lifted off my shoulders. What a rollercoaster!... And I don't like rollercoasters.

As soon as my body started to eventually calm down and get under control; I started to question myself again! Did I do ok? Everyone seemed to laugh, was that a good thing or a bad thing? Did everyone like it? Aaaaahhhh! I hope I didn't make a complete ass of myself in front of a hundred people! It was like being on a rollercoaster, sitting down and thinking "well I did it, that wasn't so bad." The difference being that I had no idea if it was actually good or bad, no one came up to me and said it was awful, does that mean it was good?

I was convinced I did terribly despite no proof of it.

Despite what I was telling myself, I got myself a drink of water, watched the last few speakers including a TEDx speaker -which made me feel like I did even worse- and I walked out. I felt like I was the worst in the room, the worst speaker there and the worst speaker ever! I beat myself up all the way to the train because I had the combination of possibly missing my train, being tired and thinking I did a terrible job of my talk. Once I'd got on the train and knew all I had to go was get off at the right stop, I managed to calm myself down, breathe -the walk helped me get rid of some of the anxiety which helped- and I wanted to try to let what had just happened sink in.

Once I felt like my head had had enough of beating me up, convincing me I was the worst person ever for putting myself through that and that I was the worst speaker ever; I started to slowly switch the more rational part of me on... the part of me that's calmer and that convinced me to do this in the first place. As soon as I started to go from screaming at myself to a much more relaxed way of talking to myself, everything started to change again and I started to think more positively.

Despite this, I still felt very embarrassed by the fact I beat myself up even when I knew it was my first time and that it was never going to be amazing; I started to judge myself for the process which was never going to help. Then I thought, "The event was recorded for YouTube!" which made me feel worse because it was public; but I then had the thought of...

what if I'm wrong? What if the way I thought it went wasn't actually the case? I did have a Facebook group at the time and I thought I'd see what others thought of the talk. So I found the URL to the talk and put it up in the group. I got comments that I was unprepared for; saying that they couldn't tell I was nervous and that the talk was really informative and even funny in parts too. As hard as it was to believe, I started to feel relief that I was proved wrong -that I didn't do as bad as I thought- which convinced me to give it another try in an attempt to do better next time.

## LESSONS FROM MICHAEL

A couple of days after the talk -and processed everything from the roller coaster week before all the way to the thinking I did horribly and positive feedback from my audience- a lot started to come up for me.

**I realised that there's nothing quite like challenging yourself for needing to practice what you preach.** It's so easy to be calm, reasonably stress free and feel good when you're comfortable and don't step outside your comfort zone. So many times I've seen people preach the idea of mindset and psychology but they never seem to really test themselves or do anything scary for them. Coming at this -not from theory- but from actually doing something that's completely far and beyond what I even dreamt I could do forced me to do things to make sure I could handle it. The phrase, "saying something a thousand times, isn't as powerful as doing it once" springs to mind and It's completely true.

**Stress and nerves were the test.** I learned the theory, I knew it inside and out, but doing something truly frightening to me taught me how to use it and what it's like to do something even when every single part of me wanted to say no and stop me. **The power of acting scared.** My led legs walking up the stairs, having to convince myself that walking on stage was a good idea was a real thing I had to do; I had to have that conversation with myself right before I was supposed to give my talk.

**Doing this taught me that I'm way stronger than I thought**, far more capable than I ever imagined and It taught me the value of me leading the way, me changing the world my way so I could show others what it actually takes -not just in theory- but by actually doing it. Everything around being on stage taught me the true value of mindset and I was actually proud of the fact that I was able to do this so I could experience exactly what it was like.
**Everything is easy until you're**

**uncomfortable** and putting myself in situations where I HAD to practice what I preached, to lead, and show others what's possible, became my life after this moment.

Once I started to think about the lessons I learned and even the possible good things that could come out of this -the fact I actually did it and that I didn't do as bad as I thought I did- I decided I was going to give it another try. I booked onto the next event which was three months away and prepared the same as I did for the first one -presentation slides and all- and did my thing.

## Public Speaking Round 2

I decided to get back out there because I learned a heck of a lot from the first time despite being so anxious and filled with worry that I didn't fully remember what I said. I wanted to see if the second time round might be better in my own head and match up more to how well others thought I did. I did keep going with the videos and did as many as I could; I noticed I was better, could form my sentences more clearly and felt like I could "just do it" without a lot of pre overthinking.

**A week before** I found myself feeling much more relaxed; almost like just the simple fact that I had already been on the stage before helped me calm down and I was able to easily think more clearly about my talk. I felt more prepared even though I actually wasn't -which felt weird- because I was essentially at the same point but the way it felt to me was different, ready, calmer, "grounded" and much more positive. When I rehearsed my talk the timings were better than before. My whole self talk around it was, "I've already done this before, so I should easily be able to do it again."

Despite that, I understood that maybe I will do better because I'm in this space and that I still do the same things I did last time; So I still meditated, walked, listened to music, the gym, yoga and stretching along with everything else I did leading up to the day of the talk. I got better results from what I did because my mental state started from a calmer place.

**On the day** I was definitely less stressed; I found myself being more social with the other speakers and attendees and not just keeping to myself. I made conversation with a couple of people which actually helped me settle in even more and felt more "at home" at the event. Much more comfortable.

This was a good thing because this time I thought I'd give a talk on my conditions and how they actually helped me personally; so as you can probably tell I needed the extra comfort-ness and confidence this time round.

**During the talk**, my heart rate was slow enough so that I could focus on what I was saying. I did feel like I could have some control over my breathing too but I was still shaking and sweating due to nerves. Because I could control my breathing, I could speak clearer, not get too anxious and actually regulate my nerves eventually. I came off feeling better, much happier with how I did. What's funny was someone that saw me at the previous event and this time round noticed I was more confident and asked me if I'd practiced more as my timings were much better -I actually practiced less- but I said thank you and that I'm glad I improved on my last talk.

Inside my I was telling myself, "WOW positive feedback there and then" which felt amazing because last time I didn't get that; what else happened that was very surreal for me was I had -not one- but two others coming up to me that said that really resonated with my talk, they too had "invisible" conditions and they could really relate to me... which felt awkward and cool at the same time.

**After the talk** I felt a sense of relief and actually said to myself, "I can do this." I had a slower walk back to the train -didn't rush as I wanted to process the moment- and it was on my way back home that I really started to see myself doing this more often.

## LESSONS FROM THE SECOND TIME

**That the first time is always the worst either physically or mentally** because it's brand new, different and you have no way of knowing how it'll look and you'll spend most of your time adapting and reacting to the situation and how you feel in that situation. It's ok for your first time to be horrible.

**Letting yourself improve** would only have been a lesson if I had dusted myself down and understood that "next time will be better." If you do something once and decide that it was horrible and that you're never going to do that again, there's no way of actually getting to the point where you improve or at least feel better in yourself about doing whatever it is you're doing. It was a combination of getting comfortable, feeling more confident and improving from last time that actually made the second talk better.

**Your mind can make it feel worse that it actually is** which did happen the first time I stepped on stage. I thought I did horribly -that I was the worst in the room- and that I should never even get on stage again... I embarrassed myself. I had the outside feedback that made me see and put the idea in my head that maybe a second time would be much better. It was after the second time that I realised that it was mostly in my head and that I could actually get up on stage and speak. It took a lot less mentally for me to go up there a second time because I had the idea in my mind that it was just my mind playing tricks on me and that I should get up there again.

**Get comfortable enough to focus on the skill** is something that most don't actually tell you; the first time on stage was so nerve wracking and emotional for me that I couldn't actually remember what I said, or how to improve; but the second time on stage I felt like I could focus on the actual skill of speaking. I felt myself thinking, processing what I wanted to say before I was saying it, and felt much more in control of myself and the situation.

It was a combination of wanting to be a speaker in the first place which pushed me to do this once, twice and more times before I actually decided to keep doing this. **Don't use your first or second time to decide if you should keep doing it** because remembering that consistency is key and that you need to get an outside honest opinion about things. You don't want to delude yourself into thinking you're better than you are or think that you're worse than you are too. Be real, positive and understand that if you "want it" from the beginning -like me- you'll find a way to do all the things I mentioned above.

Overall, the first few times I ever spoke on stage were some of the most stressful and emotional times of my life. They tested me in ways I didn't even know I could be tested and forced me to practice what I preached mindset wise. Saying something a thousand times is nothing compared to doing it once; I showed myself the power of taking action and I hope I showed you too.

## **Finding Meaning Again**

When you hear others talk about losing their purpose or any kind of meaning in their life, often it can seem scripted or that it was something they could easily course correct from and move forwards. Unfortunately -for me- it happened without me realising it and took me a while before actually doing the work I needed to do before then carrying on with my life.

Before I dive into what I needed to do in order to find meaning in my life again, I want to talk to you about one of the most influential people in my life; my grandma.

I always remember the fun I used to have growing up; my gran would come up with these crazy stories and games that would keep me occupied whenever I would visit. "Floor is lava" was one of the games I'd end up playing

-decades before everyone seemed to play it" with cushions on the floor that I would use to get from one side of the room to the other. I remember having three cushions; one behind me, one id stand on, and another in front of me and I would constantly need to move the cushions if I was going to get to the chair or the table for food -as an example- and she would always have something ready for me that she had spent ages preparing before we arrived. My gran would look forward to seeing us -me and my brother- and it would show in what she did.

As I got older she would mention things like. "You'll be able to look after me when you're rich and famous" which was something I brushed off and would have a chuckle about as if it didn't mean anything. As I started to do things like become a tennis coach and personal trainer, she would always support me, be happy and encourage me to keep chasing things I wanted while always mentioning the same phrase every so often.

When I started the online business and shared things like my article features and interviews on Sky and other things; she would always congratulate me -I'd see she was genuinely happy for me- and would encourage me to keep going. She was always in my corner.

Over the years, my gran became more and more unwell, frequent visits to the hospital and would often struggle; things took a turn when she fell one time which I don't think she ever fully recovered from. It was hard to see this happening to my gran without being able to do anything about it. Not being able to help was really tough for me.

Fast forward to me deciding to go on the fearful journey of moving abroad; which took me a while to convince my family that it's what I wanted to do -including my gran that wasn't afraid to tell me she didn't want me to go- but eventually they accepted it once I'd gave them the date and started to prepare myself for the move. Once they realised that no matter what they said, I was moving away, I think they started to be ok with the idea. Knowing that my gran didn't want me to go didn't make it easy for me; I didn't really want to leave my family behind anyway -I questioned myself before, during and even after moving- but the fact that they weren't one hundred percent behind me made much harder to convince myself that it was a good idea.

But I did it -I moved abroad- which was a huge moment for me and the life that I live today. After a few months I got some news that would change my life forever. Unfortunately she passed away.

I was in Gran Canaria at the time which was where I was living; her daughter rang me and It was random as she doesn't usually ring. I picked up the phone and when she told me, it crushed me -for about fifteen minutes- as I'd let myself feel it. One of the biggest things I'd learned over the years was to let yourself feel things rather than bottle them up, so I did. I cried as soon as I got off the phone -needed to sit down for a while- and I rang my mother to see how everyone else took the news and organised the funeral arrangements.

After everything was said and done and back home -I felt this weight lift- but what was after that was... nothing. I started to "wander" a little and suddenly felt like I had no direction in my life at all. I would gradually take longer and longer to get out of bed in the mornings, I would find myself not eating as much and had the self-talk of "nothing really matters anymore." It was almost like I had became numb to everything around my life and business, it stopped mattering if I showed up or not -aside from work with clients and businesses- but it was like the idea of creating content, recording podcasts, selling things, just stopped feeling "right" with the idea of it not mattering if I did anything or not.

Picture WHY in big letters hovering over every thought or feeling, that's what it was like for me; and I think the unemotional element also made it hard for me to come up with any good reason for doing things which meant I found myself "going through the motions" a lot. I would always do what I needed to do business wise and they seemed to go very well -despite my complete lack of motivation- but I started to feel like there was a piece of me missing. This took me a while to recognise and also have the desire to do anything about it. Zero desire to change kept me in this loop for months.

I had completely lost meaning and purpose or any reason to go on anymore, and I had no idea that this story of "looking after my family when I was rich and famous" played such a big part in motivating me -and when it was gone- I didn't know who I'd be without that. A few days to process the emotion but I didn't think about the fact I'd attached meaning to what my Gran used to tell me.

I had to get to a place where I was open to something different; I had subconsciously lived my life based on certain rules, expectations and pressures that no longer existed and I had to be ok with that and understand that I had to build my own rules and reasons for doing what I do. Life was my canvas now and I held the brush... What was I going to do about it?

Before all that It took me a couple of weeks before I noticed that I was going through the motions -aimless- and not really doing anything with my life or business; I became lazy, bored and uninspired. For some reason I had to get to this dark place for a while before getting out of it and changing things was more desirable than staying the same. Because I didn't have the desire, I had to force it.

I had to find the answers to the questions and statements that I didn't have at the time:

What's the point anymore?
Why bother?

I could disappear and it wouldn't matter

At first, I hated the fact that I didn't have the answers; I'd spend days asking myself the same questions over and over again without any sort of reply that made sense. I'd have them written down in a notepad and I'd stare at it everyday... without an answer. Until -after days of staring at my notepad constantly- I asked myself, "what if I'm asking the wrong questions?" This made me think of something different to focus on, and shifted my way of thinking.

I started to realise that perhaps I need to do things that got me excited again and motivate me to take more action. This happened before around leaping into public speaking because I wanted to play bigger -help more people- and impact the world... I was beginning to see that this could be history repeating itself and that I needed to build a reason why that came from me, and no one else.

I had to take out distractions -listen to me and only me- which involved zero podcast listening, deleting people I followed on social media, reading no books, in order to shut everyone else's voices out of my head. It might sound a little intense -because it was- but it was needed if I was ever going to get clear on my own purpose and bring more meaning to my life and how I was going to spend my time moving forwards.

I started to ask myself these questions:

What do you look forward to doing?
What passion projects could you do just for fun?
Is there anything you could stop doing?
Anything you've stopped that you wish you hadn't?

Then things got a little weird....

Who would you need to be in order to do that?

How would you need to see yourself before you did these things?
How different is it from who you are now?

This made me think about how my identity -and how I saw myself- needed to shift if I was ever going to play at the bigger level that motivated me and lit a fire in my belly to get out of my "hole" and set the world alight again. This meant getting clearer on the values and beliefs I wanted to live by; I had to almost reinvent myself if I was going to make this happen.

**WRITER**

One of the main reasons for this was that I felt caged by the expectations, standards or pre-existing assumptions that came along with the label of a coach. Now, I realise that I do many different things, but my first shift in what I did and who I was, was becoming a published writer for the first time. I had been writing posts on social media for a while, some long, some short, but someone asked me If I'd consider writing for a magazine to: reach a bigger audience, become a writer and not just someone that posts online, and have the respect that comes along with being a writer. I was taken back by it at first because I hadn't even considered that my writing was good enough, but I said yes because the worst they say is no and then I'd just go back to what I was doing.

The first time I got published in an online magazine was the third article I actually submitted but the first little bit of "I can do this" and meant that I could actually write. The idea that I could write an article that was good enough to be featured in a magazine triggered "I'm not good enough" thoughts and filled me with confirmation bias -which involved things like taking my time with the article, taking ages to decide on the topic and never feeling like it was finished- until I got my first yes. But when I did, I started to think to myself that I was a writer which triggered a new conversation.

"Can I be a writer and a coach?" started to come into my head and cause a little confusion as to what I actually did as I held onto the idea that I could only do one thing and that was it. "Coaches can't be writers too", I thought, and that I should just stay in my lane and stick to what I know and what I'm good at. One of the most important conversations ever broke me out of my mould as soon as I realised that I can do many things -I can do anything I put my mind to- and that the only limit is my imagination. I wanted to be able to do everything -I felt the term coach was the cage- but what it actually made me realise is that I can write, and coach, and do any number of things without having to "label" myself in only one way.

The problem was, of course, that I didn't realise at the time that this crisis conversation, this moment where I questioned who I was and what I actually did, was going to happen a lot as I had only ever been a coach, you can bet I was in for quite the ride...

## SPEAKER

There was a big difference between speaking once or twice, and feeling like I could actually call myself a speaker... and I felt like I didn't really "earn my stripes" or deserve the label of speaker. Being a public speaker was an aspirational pipe dream that started when my personal training clients get value from my story and convinced me to share more of it; I had always looked up to the likes of Anthony Robbins, Brendon Burchard, Nick Vujicic, Les Brown and many others that I idolised and looked up to. They were in the motivational and personal development industry and that's where I imagined myself being, But I felt like I had to wait until I was ready.

The next time I felt this way was when I got enough feedback about my story (the one you're reading now) and how helpful it could be to others. Just "me being me". Again, the idea that I could be valuable, inspirational and help people just by sharing my story seemed very far fetched and I simply didn't believe it. It simply couldn't be possible for me to just share my story and lessons I've learned could be even remotely valuable. I used to tell myself that I hadn't achieved anything, that I didn't have a "rags to riches" story and that I wasn't good enough to communicate my story in a way others would enjoy.

I used to watch motivational speakers and public speakers and I would compare myself to them -now I know not to and to stick to my own message- but I would do that constantly and use that to convince myself that I would never get to that level, never get to the stage where my story and how I spoke would cause a change and transformation in others. Everytime I watched them it cemented in me the idea that I was simply not good enough and that they must have been born with the gift of speaking. After decades of hiding -keeping to myself and being one of the quietest people I'd ever met- it was very easy for me to think that I couldn't do it; that it simply wasn't "me" and that somehow you had to be born with it to be able to do it. Only after learning that I could improve, after realising that -like everything else- speaking and talking is a skill and that all I had to do was learn it.

As you can tell, I had a lot of self worth and self value issues along with all the reasons possible for not becoming a motivational and public speaker; but I did it anyway which is the reason you're reading this now. As soon as I adopted the idea that I could change, what I was born with didn't have to define me or be all I have, things started to change pretty quickly for me. I started to research public speaking, how they do it, I started to practice talks and record videos that no one would see. It took me months before being on camera even felt "ok" before I started to post my videos online.

One of the biggest things I had to realise about speaking and sharing your story was this; any lesson, any adversity you've overcome, and how you did it, is valuable to someone going through something the same or similar to you. No matter how small it may seem to you -or someone else- it could mean the difference between success and failure and I started to feel a level of responsibility to those people to share it. I went one step further; I started to tell myself that I was doing a disservice to the world and the people that needed to hear my story by not sharing it. Whether it be at live events or otherwise, I felt compelled to speak and that allowed me to own the speaker part of myself. I felt I had no other choice but to serve at the highest level and speaking was how I wanted to do it.

*PODCASTER*

The story behind my show started a year before I actually launched; the idea of starting my own podcast came about from listening to podcasts and having the thought of, "I'd love to have my own podcast, it sounds great." The problem was it was a nice thing to have, not something I was actually committed to starting and being consistent with; so I didn't give it another thought for months. Each time I had the thought it would brush off and I would carry on as if nothing had happened. Then, after a few more months, it started to stick with me, it went from a nice thing to have to something that warranted reasons why I couldn't.

That's almost like step one and two of an idea becoming something to take action on, at first it's a fleeting thought, then It becomes something you have to come up with reasons why you can't. For me, I had a few excuses why I couldn't start my own podcast.

**I had this need for it to be perfect**; I needed the best equipment, so I would search for the podcast equipment my idols used and realised they had a dedicated studio for their podcasts,

165

mics, mixers, sound treated rooms, editing software and all kinds. I realised just how much went into their shows and that overwhelmed me and the cost of it all priced me out of the game completely.

**I also didn't like the sound of my own voice**; this meant that a lot of my reasons for not creating content initially resurfaced when it came to my podcast. It was a realization for me that just because you can overcome your insecurities and fears once, doesn't mean they'll never show up again.

I understood that a lot of the reason behind not starting came down to the fact that **I didn't think I was good enough to have my own show**, so I would come up with stories and excuses that were all centered around not liking myself enough to do it. This kept me stuck for most of the year. It was how I felt about myself that stopped me from showing up at the start, and it showed up again when I wanted to up my game too.

**The fact that I wanted it to be perfect right away and lack of "worthiness"** caused me to be in research mode for about six months. I went on all the courses, googling how all the other big podcasters do things and coming up with "well I can't do that" for everything I found. At least, until I listened to one podcast episode of the Joe Rogan Experience; Joe was the "king of the hill" at the time of writing this book when it came to podcasting and spoke about how he recorded his first podcasts on his iphone.

This made me think just how easy it could be if I shifted my perspective away from what I couldn't do to what I could do. I asked myself, "How could it look with what I have access to right now?". So I used my iphone, used zoom which was my recording software of choice that allowed me to record on my phone, I tested out a simple headset, liked it, and I got started.

To give my podcast the best chance of hitting the prominent lists on places like iTunes, I thought it best to have a launch period where I encourage listeners everyday. Luckily I had a few friends that wanted to be my first guests and I got a few replies to my messages. I launched with around five to ten shows being released over a two week period and we were off!

Then something crazy happened, I sent a couple of messages to people that I followed, people I admired and looked up to. I thought to myself, "well, you never know, but they probably won't reply." Similar to a lot of things in the past, I accepted that it probably wouldn't go well, but I did it anyway. The craziest thing happened… they replied and said that they would love to be a guest on my podcast! The best way I can describe how I felt was, "OMG OMG OMG OMG OMG!" I couldn't believe it; it was a combination of shock, disbelief and a little bit of denial too. "There's no way this is real!" started to play in my head, my hands shaking, heart pounding -I nearly dropped my phone- when I slowly typed, "That's great! How would you like to book your space?"

So I had interviews, I was recording shows, sharing episodes, the launch went pretty well; but then I realised I had to keep going now. I had to figure out a way of running my podcast long term and that was a challenge for me and after 6 months I wanted to quit. I was struggling to get guests and I actually started to not be motivated and enjoy everything that comes along with running a podcast. I realised that I didn't start with the long term in mind and took steps like having specific days to record amongst other things gave me the space I needed to enjoy the show again.

At this point I started to see the podcast as more than just a hobby -more than just a passion project- and asked myself just how far I can take this. Once I'd overcame the initial "growing pains" things started to go well. I didn't consider myself a podcaster because I felt it came with a lot of responsibility, professionalism and a level of commitment that I didn't feel ready for. Until something changed…

When I interviewed my first ever celebrity, I realised just how much more work on myself I needed to do. I sent messages almost hoping they wouldn't get back to me -definitely a hit and hope strategy at the time- and I convinced myself that it wouldn't happen… much like the other things that I've pitched for. It was different because when it comes to having guests on your podcast, some people mean more to me than others. There are famous people that no one knows about and there are -shall we say- less famous people that you idolise and have followed for years; that's what this was for me. The difference of course was that this person was also seen as a celebrity in the industry and when they agreed to be a guest on the podcast, you can bet I had a hard time accepting it and feeling ok with being in this situation in general.

Same spirals as last time and even though I'd been through them many times before -and had the strategies ready to go for managing it- I still had to go through it.

"Oh my god, oh my god, oh my god!"
"I can't believe it"
"Why did they say yes?!"
"I can't do this!"

They were just some of the things that were running through my mind at the time and I had to work heavily on breathing slowly and grounding myself before I could even carry on with my day, nevermind handling the interview. But we confirmed -I cleared the rest of my diary for that day- and it was a case of getting back to work as it was around two months away. I had to tell myself that "everything was ok, I had plenty of time to prepare and I'll do a good job."

I did my best to just treat it like any other interview -even though it wasn't- so I tried not to think about it until on the day -which I failed at as from about a week before it was almost all I could think about-, did my usual research -which wasn't really needed as I followed them already- and as you could probably guess, I couldn't switch my brain off. I couldn't get over the fact that I had this interview and I had the thought of "I can't do this, what the hell am I doing?! This doesn't happen to people like me" on repeat for an entire week; I slept less and less, was more and more anxious and I tried to spend more and more time on things like self care and meditating just to take the edge off.

Luckily I had the day-to-day going on with my businesses which did help take my mind off it; which meant that it only really "bubbled over" when I had time to myself or generally before I would go to sleep. So I either kept my mind busy or meditated or did something to help me manage the voice that was playing on repeat in my head.

I had booked the whole day off so I could focus on only essential business activities and the interview; self care was a priority so I was in the best state I could be in for the interview. I went on walks and worked out, listened to my favourite music playlists along with focusing on keeping my breathing slow. Did it help? Definitely, but I still had to process the anxiousness, the excitement and realise that being nervous is normal given the situation.

The interview was a bit of a blur and a rush mentally; I felt myself getting so anxious and worked up that I forgot what to say -luckily I had made notes- but I managed to ground myself again and just get through it. Afterwards there was a sense of not "coming down from the high" as I was so emotional; it took me about an hour or two after the interview to actually feel like I could relax. "I did it, I actually did it!" I thought as I sat there and decided to take my show more seriously from now on. Everything from the promotions of each episode and how much time I'd spend attracting and reaching out to potential celebrity guests. I decided that this wouldn't be a "one off thing" and that I wanted to get used to the feeling of being in front of influencers and celebrities.

It felt strange that it would start initially with me -my level of commitment- before I started to feel good about calling myself a podcaster. After that, I started to write articles and be interviewed on podcasting; people asking me for help to start and grow their own shows along with my own show growing in popularity started off surreal for me but became more and more comfortable as time went on. I started to be more committed and earn the title before it felt like I deserved it.

## INSPIRATION BY JUST BEING MYSELF

I had spent my entire life being a coach; from tennis, to health and fitness, and mindset. I enjoyed coaching -helping people is what I was passionate about- but over time I started to feel like I was drawn to something more. I was drawn to the idea of helping people because it made me feel great and positively impacting lives -changing the world- is why I feel I was put here on this planet. Similar to the moment I decided it was time to play bigger than tennis and fitness to take my message online, it started to become clear to me that I was growing away from the idea of just being a coach. Nothing against this if this is something you do and want to stick with but I felt drawn to the idea of being more.

The idea of being an inspirational figure started with my story helping my clients at the gym and became something that started to take shape the more I put myself out there; but I never really thought of myself as an inspirational person -it's something others would say to me- which meant that it took me longer to accept. This was the thing to remember -it wasn't about me and what I thought of myself as- it was more about other people and how they saw me and my ability to accept that it was happening to me to a certain degree and I had to be ok with that.

At first, I brushed it off; I didn't agree with them and I downplayed what It meant. I almost ignored it if I'm being completely honest. Thoughts like, "it doesn't matter what they think" and, "surely that isn't right" was common for me; I held onto the labels I wanted to have or those that I agreed with -because it meant I could stay in my bubble and not "upgrade" how I showed up- all before I realised that I couldn't control it. As much as I wanted to control how others saw me, I had to be ok with other people thinking of me as something that makes sense to them.

Whether it's coach, podcaster, inspirational, writer or even author; I had to embrace the fact that while what others think of me doesn't matter as much as what I thought of myself, I also had to be ok with others thinking of me in a particular way. Inspiration was what they thought of me and **I couldn't let other people's opinions of me hold me back or change how I showed up;** instead, I had to use that as a motivation to step into that role rather than shy away from it.

## BIGGEST LESSONS AS AN INTROVERT

**Performing is a skill, just like everything else.** Even though I am a quiet person and very introverted, does that really mean I can't be on camera, stage or tv? When I read examples of introverts being on stage or being performers it made me think that maybe they found a way. Being an introvert didn't define them and I had to learn that it didn't define me either. Your circumstances or conditioning don't define you unless you let them.

**Sometimes you have to create the situations then meet the expectations by being who you need to be in order to succeed.** I can't tell you how many times I would shy away from doing something, but when I jumped first -set the dates and commitments- I found a way to make it work and handle it. Speaking on stage was to set the date then figure out the situation as with many of the other things I've achieved. Creating the situations always works out better than wishing or waiting because it involves taking action and being proactive. Which as introverts it can be easy to not do, even though we need to.

**Acting scared can be the only way**, sometimes you don't have any choice. When people say "you can get through this" they tend to brush over the fact that you're going to feel bad -it is going to freak you out- and you're likely going to have to do what you can while you're scared. Do you run away or lean into the fear and worry you feel? Getting through it means feeling the fear and doing it anyway but you may have to do it scared too.

**It takes more effort and more action than you think** and most of the results you see are created behind the scenes. The many articles you send the events you apply to speak at, the podcasts you apply to be a guest on… without a reply. Then sooner or later, you get replies, you start to get yes's and you wonder if the many repetitions you do every day or week are worth it. They are -all of them- because over time you become amazing and eventually, they can't NOT notice you.

**It can be so easy to want to stay safe and be in control** and as an introvert that was my resting state; being quiet and not really being visible at all was a place where I had the most control over my life and business. It was "normal" for me to do the bare minimum and get by and the danger was that it was slowly becoming easy and desirable to stay that way. But when you're called upon for more and have this deep feeling of wanting to impact the world, that was enough for me to go on this journey and redefine for myself what normal was. Finding something that motivates you to be visible can change everything for you.

**There's a difference between being extroverted and being confident**. Being an introvert looks a certain way and If you want to be visible, maybe you have to "turn it on" instead of having it be your resting state. If you see yourself as a confident person, that shows up a certain way which may be different for you as an introvert compared to an extrovert and that's something I had to embrace; maybe you do too?

**"The world doesn't need another anyone else, the world just needs the first you!"**

Have you watched "Fighting With My Family"? I'm a big Rock fan so of course I loved the film but there's actually a deeper lesson hidden within it, The Rock mentions that the wrestling world doesn't need another him, he wasn't another one of anyone else he was the first him.

And the lesson is relevant here, I used to think I had to be someone else, another Gary Vee for example. But I'm not him and neither are you and that's ok. We don't need to be.

## How Could Being Visible Look For You

Being an introvert doesn't mean you can't be visible, in fact some of the biggest names in the world are introverts. Some people find "putting a mask on" helps -some find becoming someone different works- but you may be like me and find that being true to who you are is the best way of making the most of your visibility and using this almost as a form of self discovery. Over the years I've realized things about myself that I never would have without starting this journey. It was so easy for me to just settle for things and "it is what it is" moments forming the majority of my life.

Once I felt the pull of feeling like I was destined for more -once I believed I was worthy of something greater than simply going through the motions- I realised I had to change, grow and find out about myself at the same time. Maybe that's the same for you?

Maybe you're "stuck in a rut" -lacking motivation, direction and purpose- because you've accepted that your past is your present becomes your future and because you're quiet -introverted- and perhaps never really put yourself out there before... you don't think you can.

Let this book give you hope; a realization that you can act scared and that you don't need to back off just because things are difficult. My hope with the book is that it gives you the feeling of "I'm not alone, this is normal, Mike went through this and kept going; so can I" and that you follow through with what you say you're going to do more often because you read this book.

## Join The Community!

I have a FREE community on Facebook for introverted entrepreneurs and changemakers that want to put themselves out there BUT have fears and insecurities that make it impossible for them to do it!

Join me in the Introverts Impacting Millions Facebook group!

## *Want To Go Above & Beyond?*

Message to Millions is where you get to work with me 1-2-1 and create your legacy ecosystem as an introvert and give you the tools, strategies and mindset to positively impact the world!

There's Limited spaces yearly so message me on social media to apply!

# ABOUT THE AUTHOR

Michael Brian McDonnell (AKA Mike McDonnell, Michael Brian) is an award winning entrepreneur, philanthropist, coach, podcaster, speaker and author. Michael specialises in helping introverts have their message, business and passion seen so they can impact millions and leave a lasting legacy.

Michael Brian McDonnell is available for speaking engagements and interviews.

@TheMichaelBrian on social media

# Michael Brian Foundation

The Michael Brian Foundation believes having a brighter future means investing in the potential of our younger generations!

Through funding, mentoring and more we can empower those that would otherwise be forgotten about the opportunity to impact the world in a positive way.

You can find out more about the work The Michael Brian Foundation does over at: www.michaelbrianfoudation.org

Printed in Great Britain
by Amazon